my big animal world

Barbara Taylor

priddy books
big ideas for little people

About this book

Children love learning about the amazing animals that populate our world. My Big Animal World takes them on a unique journey, introducing them to hundreds of animals while exploring the diverse range of environments in which they live. Looking at how they adapt to their habitats, and discovering their surprising, often amusing habits brings these intriguing creatures to life. With its easy-to-turn spiral binding, this book is a great reference tool for school projects or homework. Adults, too, will gain a fascinating insight into the lives of the many animals with whom we share our amazing world.

Written by: Barbara Taylor
Editorial by: Simon Mugford and Hermione Edwards
Design by: Emma Surry

175 Fifth Avenue, New York, NY 10010

Created for St. Martin's Press by
priddy books

Manufactured in Malaysia

Contents

Animal habitats
Pages 8-9

Mountains
Pages 10-11

Wetlands
Pages 12-15

Forests
Pages 16-19

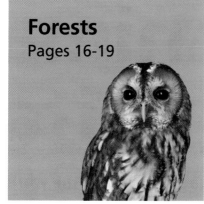

Rainforests
Pages 20-25

Grasslands
Pages 26-29

Deserts
Pages 30-33

Islands
Pages 34-35

Coral reefs
Pages 36-37

Oceans
Pages 38-41

Polar areas
Pages 42-45

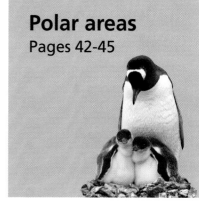

Our habitat
Pages 46-49

Animals in danger
Pages 50-53

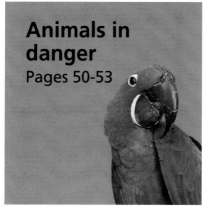

Amazing animals
Pages 54-57

Glossary
Pages 58-59

Index
Pages 60-61

Animal habitats

Animals live all over the world, in icy polar areas and cold forests as well as in baking hot deserts and steamy rainforests. The place where an animal lives is called its habitat, and each habitat has its own typical mixture of animals. The greatest variety of animals live in forest habitats, particularly in the rainforests. Only a few animals can survive in extreme habitats, such as deserts and mountains.

Mountains
Mountain tops are cold, windy places, similar to polar areas. Large birds of prey, such as eagles, are common in mountain habitats. Birds of prey can fly well in the strong mountain winds.

Wetlands
Wetland habitats, such as rivers, lakes and swamps, give food and shelter to animals in many different parts of the world. Wetland animals, such as otters, are good swimmers.

In the large, open spaces of grasslands, lions usually live together in groups called prides

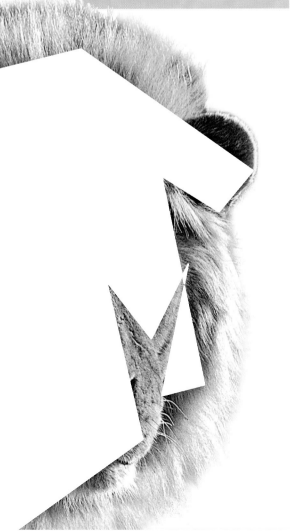

Islands
Cut off from the main land areas of the world, islands are often home to some very strange animals, from giant tortoises to the fearsome Komodo dragon.

Forests

Forest habitats are found in the areas between the cold polar regions at either end of the globe, and the hot desert and rainforest areas around the middle. Owls are common forest animals.

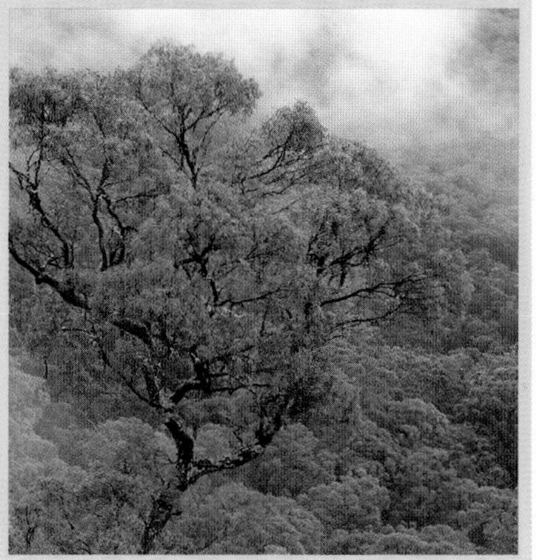

Rainforests

Growing around the middle of the world, rainforests are warm all year round because they receive plenty of heat from the Sun. It is easy for animals to survive in the rainforests.

Grasslands

Grasslands grow mainly around the edges of rainforests and deserts. They are warm or hot habitats, and usually have both wet and dry seasons. Many grazing animals live here.

Deserts

Hardly any rain falls in deserts, and animals have to cope with dry conditions and extreme temperatures. Camels are desert animals, but many small animals live in underground burrows.

Coral reefs

Coral reefs can only form in warm oceans, because this is where the tiny coral animals that make up the reef grow. Many different animals feed among the corals, including colorful fish.

Oceans

The ocean is the biggest habitat in the world. It covers about 70 per cent of the globe. Shoreline animals, such as crabs, have to be tough as they are exposed to both air and pounding waves.

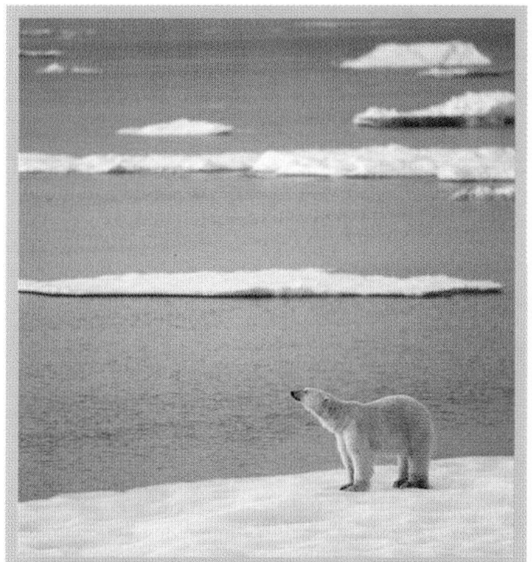

Polar areas

The polar areas at the top and bottom of the world receive less heat and light from the Sun than other parts of the world. Only very hardy animals survive the cold temperatures and winds.

Our habitat

Though we may not always be aware of them, animals surround us wherever we live – in cities as well as in the countryside. People keep animals as pets, as well as for food and wool.

Mountains

High up on mountain tops, the weather is very cold and windy, as it is in polar areas. Thick fur or feathers keep animals warm. Some animals sleep through the cold winter months, while others move down the mountain to warmer places.

Hot baths

Japanese macaques are clever monkeys. They have learned to keep warm in winter by sitting in the hot water gushing out of volcanic springs in the mountains.

Leaping cat

The powerful snow leopard uses its long back legs to make huge leaps from rock to rock. Its big paws and strong claws help it grip slippery rocks, and its long tail helps with balance on steep mountain slopes. The snow leopard's feet have furry soles, so it can walk on snow without sinking in.

LOCATION

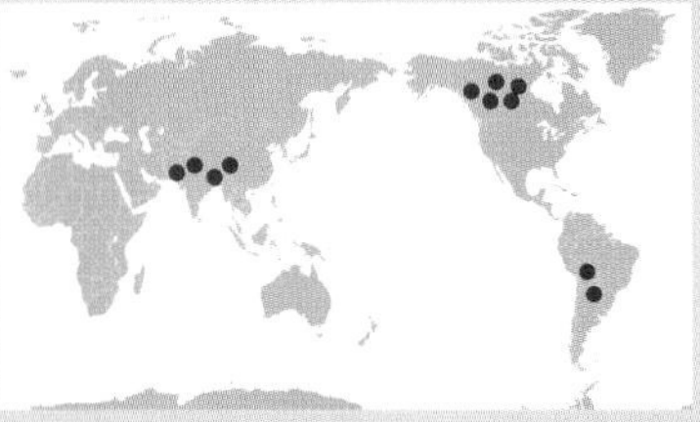

Climate
The temperature drops by about 33°F for every 500 feet you climb, so the tops of mountains are often covered in snow

Habitat
Many mountain plants have hairy leaves to trap warmth and moisture, and brightly colored flowers that attract insects

Earthwatch
Cutting down mountain forests allows soil and water to wash down the mountains, causing more floods and mudslides

Cows with skirts

A long hairy 'skirt' of fur keeps a yak's legs warm. Despite their large size, yaks are nimble, and are good at climbing the steep mountain slopes. In Nepal and Tibet, people keep yaks as farm animals. They use them for carrying heavy loads up and down the mountains, and also drink their milk.

Playful panda

Giant pandas live in the mountain forests of China, where there is lots of snow in winter. They love to play in the snow! Luckily, giant pandas have thick, waterproof fur, which keeps them warm and dry. Pandas are good at climbing trees. Their strong, curved claws help them grip tree trunks and branches.

Rock climber

The agile Rocky Mountain goat has hollows under its hooves that work like suction cups to grip rocks firmly. It is sure-footed, able to climb up steep rock faces and run along slippery slopes. This allows the goat to find food and avoid predators.

Sky hunter

Eagles, such as bald eagles, glide over mountain slopes, using their sharp eyes to look for prey, such as rabbits and birds. They have wide, powerful wings, and can fly well even in strong winds. They can also float on the air that rises up the mountains, which saves flapping their wings and wasting energy.

Fur coat

Wild chinchillas live high up in the Andes Mountains of South America, but they are also kept as pets. Chinchillas have very thick, soft fur to keep out the cold. Many of them have been killed for their fur, which is used to make coats and jackets.

The chamois of Europe can leap more than 20 feet forward and around 6 feet into the air

At 29,028 feet, Mount Everest in the Himalayas is the highest mountain on Earth

Snow leopards can bring down prey more than three times their own size

The huge condor of the Andes mountains of South America can soar through the sky for hours without flapping its wings

Wetlands

Wetlands provide plenty of food and shelter for a huge range of animals, especially the young of animals such as insects, frogs and fish. Enormous numbers of birds, such as flamingos and herons, nest in wetlands. Many water animals are good swimmers and have webbed feet to push them through the water easily.

White horses

These beautiful white horses live on marshlands in southern France. They are very hardy, and are able to survive hot summers and cold winters with little food to eat. Their wide hooves stop them sinking into the soft mud. The survival of these horses is threatened by the drainage and pollution of their marshland home.

LOCATION

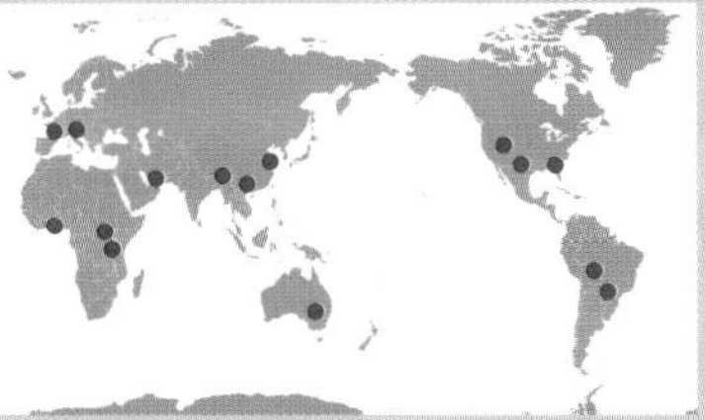

Climate
Different types of wetlands exist in areas with varying climates, and they are sensitive to changes in local conditions

Habitat
Wetlands cover about 6 per cent of the world. They include rivers, lakes and ponds, as well as marshes, swamps and bogs

Earthwatch
Wetlands help control flooding and pollution, and protect coasts from storms. Many have already been destroyed

Underwater hunter

Otters swim underwater in rivers, hunting for fish and crayfish. To swim slowly, the otter moves its webbed feet up and down in a doggy-paddle movement. To move faster, the otter holds its legs close to its sides, and bends its whole body up and down. The powerful tail acts as a rudder to help the otter steer and change direction.

Paddling along

The rare manatee has a large, rounded tail, which pushes it through the water at speeds of 15 mph. It can stay underwater for up to 15 minutes, but has to come to the surface to breathe air. Its nostrils are on the tip of its snout so it can breathe easily from the surface. Manatees munch through 165 pounds of water plants in a day.

Open wide

A hippopotamus often threatens a rival by opening its mouth very wide to show off its big teeth. Hippos are very good swimmers, and can stay underwater for up to five minutes. They spend most of the day resting in lakes or rivers, and come out at night to munch the grass on lake shores or river banks.

Castle home

Beavers build a home of sticks in the middle of a pond, which they create by building a dam across a river. This home is like a castle surrounded by a moat, and is called a lodge. It helps keep predators away. Baby beavers, called kits, are born in the safety of the lodge, which has underwater entrances.

Eggs or babies?

The platypus of Australia is an extremely unusual mammal, because it lays eggs, rather than giving birth to babies like most other mammals. It has a sensitive bill, which it uses to feel for prey at the bottom of lakes and rivers. Platypuses have no teeth, so they have to crush their food between hard, ridged plates inside their bill.

Lake Baikal in Siberia is the deepest lake in the world. It contains more freshwater than North America's five Great Lakes combined

Some beaver dams are over 328 feet long and are as tall as a person. A beaver only takes ten minutes to chew down a small tree

The Amazon river is the second longest river in the world, and holds more than one-fifth of the Earth's freshwater

American alligators were once rare, but numbers are increasing. Alligators bred in captivity have been released into the wild

Snap happy

Crocodiles lurk under the water of rivers, lakes and swamps, waiting to snap up fish and other prey in their huge jaws and sharp teeth. Crocodiles have two or three times as many teeth as an adult human. These teeth keep growing, so if a tooth falls out, a new one grows through to replace it. A crocodile's teeth are not good for chewing food, so they have to swallow food whole, or tear it into chunks.

Diving jewels

To catch fish, a kingfisher dives straight down into the water, with its shiny feathers sparkling in the light. It uses its dagger-like bill to spear a fish, then carries it back to a perch above the water. After beating the fish against a hard surface, the kingfisher swallows it down whole. Kingfishers lay their eggs in tunnels that they dig in riverbanks.

Stilt legs

Herons wade through deep water on their long legs, looking for fish and frogs to catch in their sharp, pointed bill. They also have long toes, which allow them to spread out their weight. This means they can walk over mud or floating plants without sinking in.

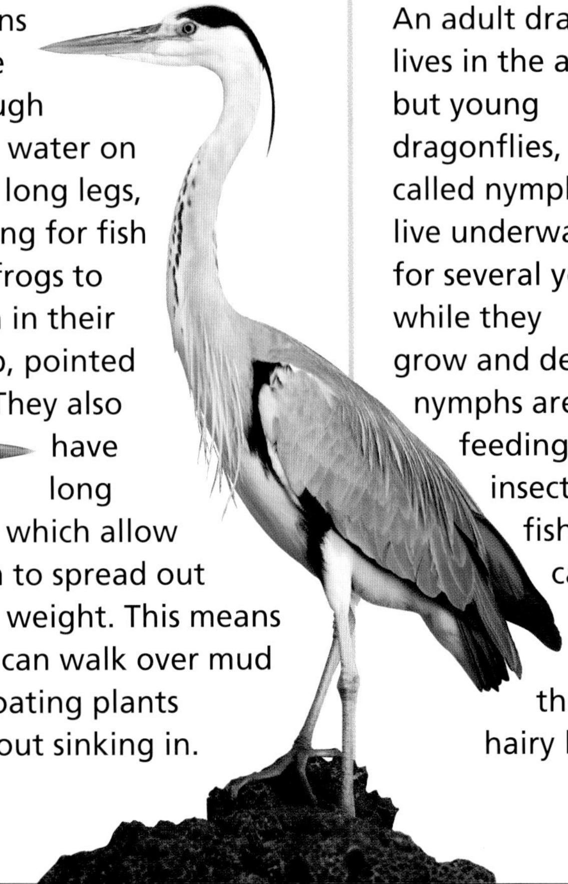

A double life

An adult dragonfly lives in the air, but young dragonflies, called nymphs, live underwater for several years while they grow and develop. The nymphs are fierce hunters, feeding on water insects and young fish. The adults catch flying insects with their hairy legs.

Bottoms up

Mallards have skin stretched between their toes, making their feet webbed. These webbed feet work like the flippers that people wear for snorkeling, and they push the ducks quickly through the water. Mallards feed on the surface, or with their bills pointing down, under the water. Their bills are wide and flat, which allows them to strain food.

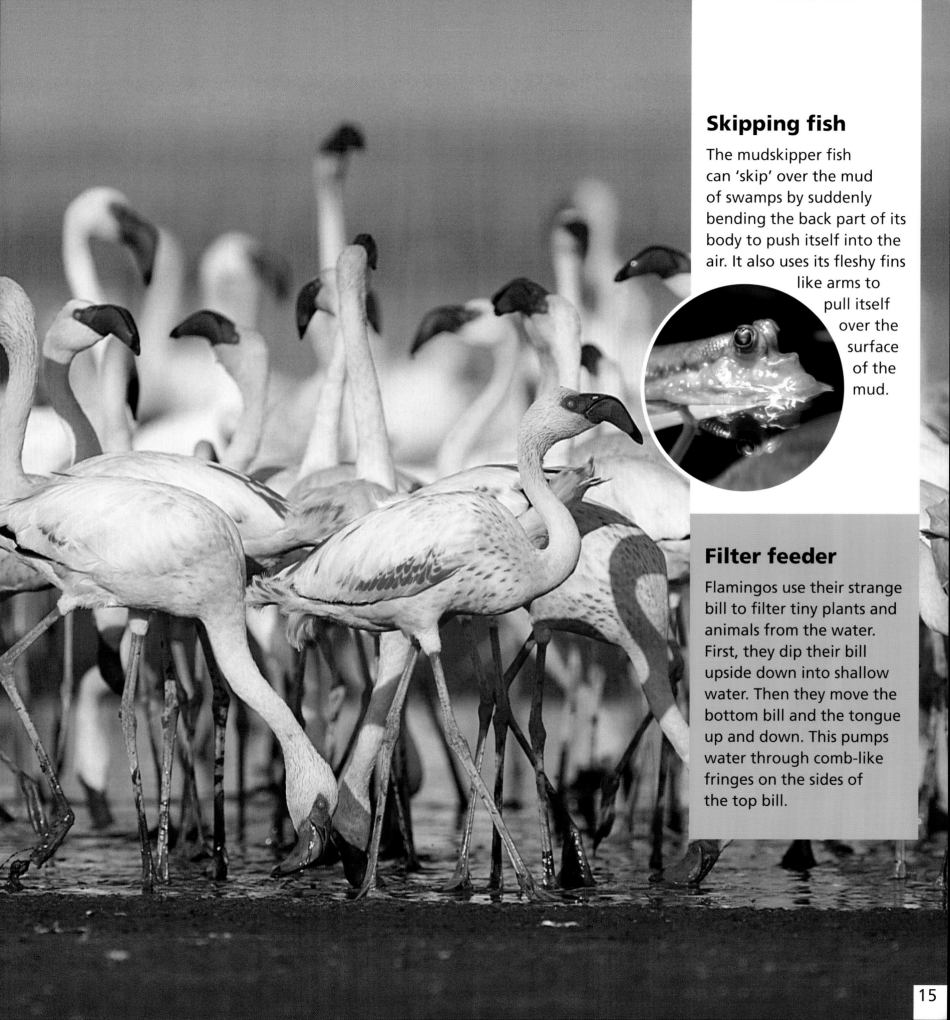

Skipping fish

The mudskipper fish can 'skip' over the mud of swamps by suddenly bending the back part of its body to push itself into the air. It also uses its fleshy fins like arms to pull itself over the surface of the mud.

Filter feeder

Flamingos use their strange bill to filter tiny plants and animals from the water. First, they dip their bill upside down into shallow water. Then they move the bottom bill and the tongue up and down. This pumps water through comb-like fringes on the sides of the top bill.

Forests

Forests and woods provide food and nesting places for a variety of animals. Their lives are closely linked to the seasons. Spring is a time for babies to be born, summer and fall are feeding and growing seasons, while winter is for resting or moving away to warmer places.

Spiny climber

Porcupines have thousands of long, very sharp spines called quills, which give them protection from predators. One porcupine may have as many as 30,000 quills! These spiny animals use their strong claws to grip tree trunks as they search for bark to eat.

Giant deer

Moose and elk are the biggest deer in the world. They are taller than a person and weigh about as much as six people! A moose uses its overhanging top lip to tear off leaves and branches. Its long legs and wide hooves allow it to wade through snow, bogs and lakes.

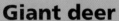

LOCATION

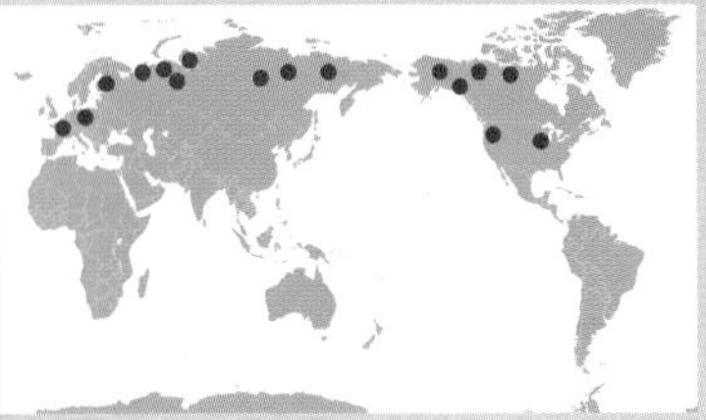

Climate
Winters in coniferous forests can last as long as eight months, with temperatures often below 32°F

Habitat
In coniferous forests, evergreen trees have leaves all year round. Deciduous trees drop their leaves in fall

Earthwatch
Pine trees can be badly damaged by acid rain, which is caused by polluting gases mixing with water in the air

Furry explorer

American black bears are intelligent and curious animals that like to explore their surroundings. They are good at climbing trees. Black bears usually live alone, except for mothers with cubs. When the cubs are born, they are so tiny that their mother is over 500 times heavier than they are!

...ave
...their coats

antlers.
The ...s fight
...ith their
antlers in the fall,
and the strongest males
win a group of females.

Tightrope walker

Red and gray squirrels move like tightrope walkers on the tree branches. They can climb and leap along the thinnest twigs, using their bushy tail to help them balance. Squirrels also flick their tail to signal to other squirrels.

Winter sleep

The dormouse survives the cold winter months by going into a deep sleep called hibernation. All its body processes slow down, and it lives off fat stored in its body during the fall.

Big ears

Long-eared bats make high-pitched squeaks and use their large ears to pick up the echoes as they bounce back from nearby objects. The echoes help the bats work out where things are so they can fly easily through the trees at night and find insects to eat.

Pack hunter

By hunting together in a group called a pack, wolves can kill large animals, such as deer and moose. Wolves have keen senses of smell and hearing to track their prey, and long legs to chase after their victims. They are the wild ancestors of the dogs people keep as pets.

The biggest area of forest in the world is the 'taiga' that stretches across the top of North America, Europe and Asia

Nutcrackers bury up to 4,000 seeds each fall to feed to their young the following spring

A large oak tree is home to as many as 300 different kinds of insects

Cork is made from the bark of cork oak trees. The bark is stripped about every ten years without damaging the tree

Twisted bill

Crossbills are named after the way the two parts of their bill cross over at the tips. This is a good shape to lift up the scales of pine cones and reach the seeds inside. The seeds are full of goodness, and adult crossbills feed the seeds to their young.

Silent swooper

Woodland owls, such as the tawny owl (left) have short, wide, rounded wings, which allow them to fly in the small spaces between the trees. Owls can fly silently because they have fluffy fringes on their soft feathers, which muffle the sound of their wingbeats. They swoop down to catch their prey in their sharp, curved claws, called talons.

Chisel bird

Woodpeckers have a pointed, sharp bill, which they use to chisel into tree trunks to find insects to eat. They lick up the insects with a very long, sticky tongue, which can be as long as their own body.

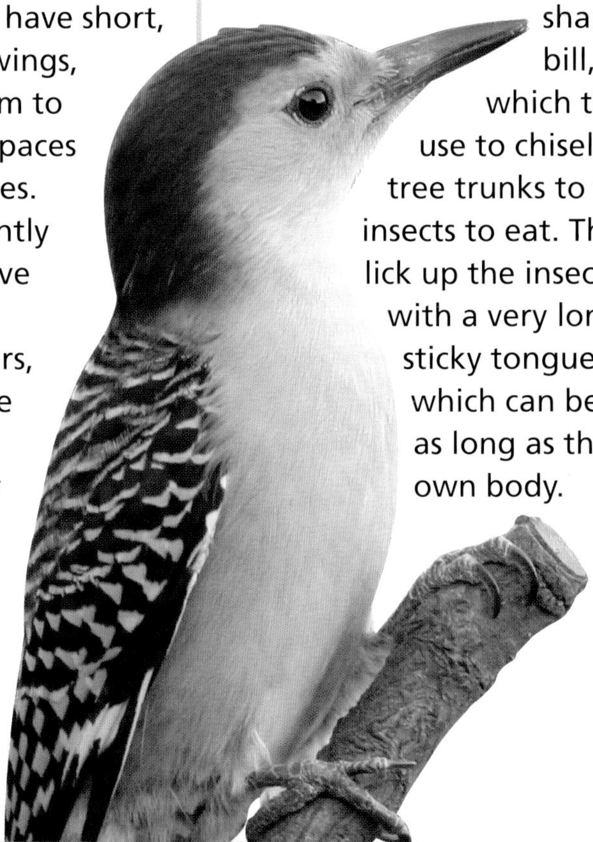

Hide-and-seek

During the day, the whip-poor-will rests among the fallen leaves on the woodland floor. Its brown mottled feathers provide good camouflage so the bird is very hard for predators to spot. At night, the whip-poor-will flies near the ground with its mouth open to scoop up insects.

Insects such as beetles are the whip-poor-will's favorite food

Fighting beetles

Stag beetles are named for the huge jaws of the males, which look like a male deer's antlers. Males use their jaws to fight rivals, rather like human wrestlers. The beetles lock their jaws together in tests of strength. They try to lift each other into the air and throw their opponent to the ground.

Tree planter

Blue jays often bury tree seeds, such as acorns, in the fall, and then dig them up to eat during the winter months. Many of the seeds are never eaten and grow into new trees, helping woodlands to spread.

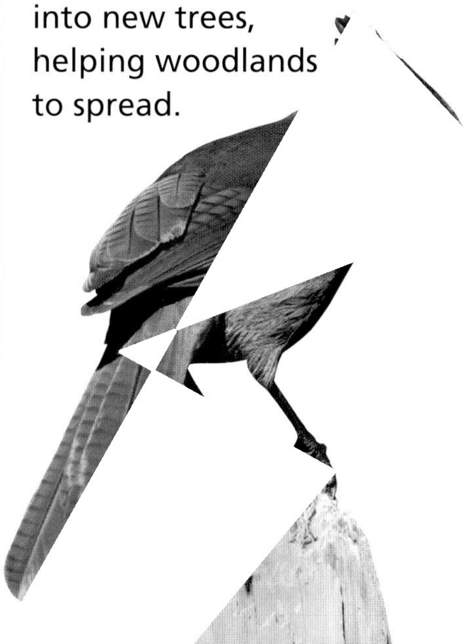

Nest thief

The female cuckoo does not make a nest of her own. Instead, she lays her eggs in other birds' nests. When the cuckoo chick hatches out of its egg, it tips the other eggs out of the nest so it has all the food and space for itself!

Monarch marathon

Monarch butterflies fly thousands of miles to escape the cold winters in Canada. They fly south to forests in Mexico, where it is warmer. As they fly, the monarch butterflies glide on the wind, without flapping their wings, to save energy on their long journey.

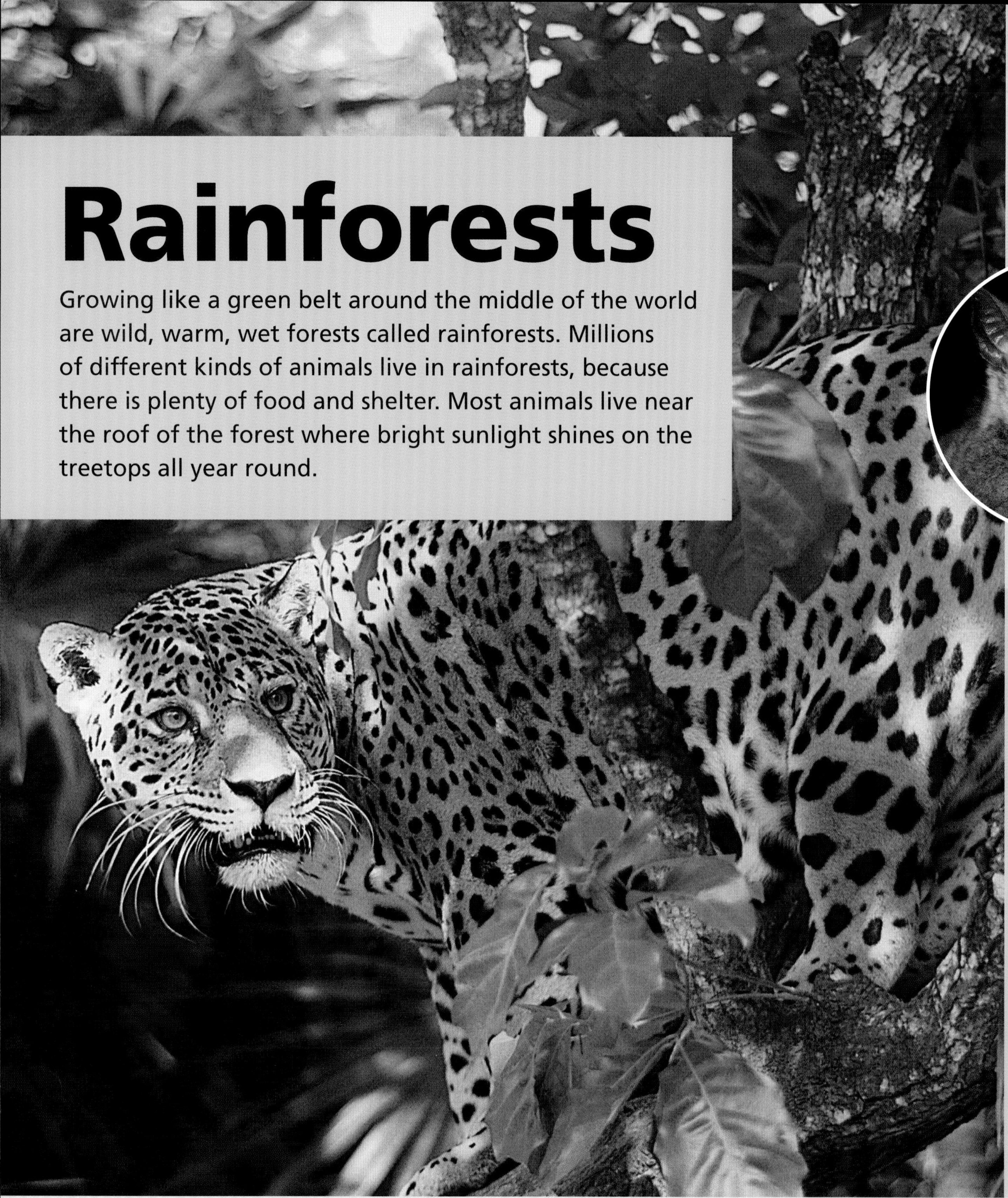

Rainforests

Growing like a green belt around the middle of the world are wild, warm, wet forests called rainforests. Millions of different kinds of animals live in rainforests, because there is plenty of food and shelter. Most animals live near the roof of the forest where bright sunlight shines on the treetops all year round.

Night senses

The huge eyes and ears of bushbabies help them catch insects in the dark. Bushbabies are named for their strange call, which sounds like the cry of a child.

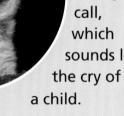

Spotted hunter

The jaguar's spotted coat allows it to hide among the leafy branches and make surprise attacks on its prey, such as wild pigs or deer. Sometimes jaguars even catch and eat crocodiles. They have very strong jaws and teeth, which can bite through bones.

LOCATION

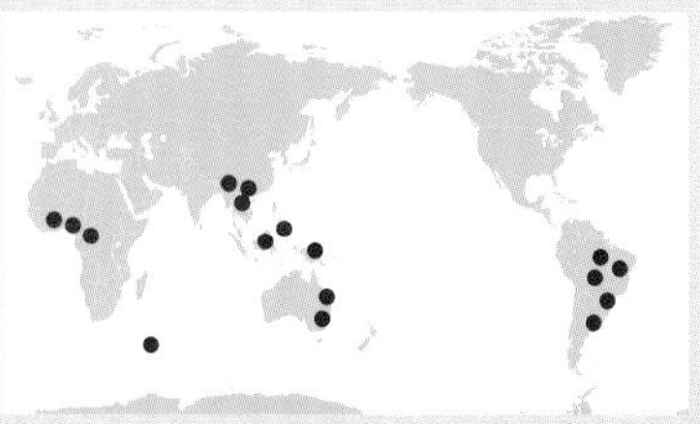

Climate
Most rainforests can get as much as 100 inches of rainfall a year – the same height as a two-story building

Habitat
A 4-square mile area of rainforest contains as many as 1,500 flowering plants and 750 species of trees

Earthwatch
About half the world's rainforests have been cut down, and an area the size of a soccer field is destroyed every second

Clever chimps

Chimpanzees are very clever animals. They chew sticks or grass stems to make a tool for catching termites. They push the tool into a termite mound and when they pull it out, the termites are clinging to the end. Few other animals make and use tools in this way.

Super swinger

Gibbons use their very long arms to swing underneath the branches of rainforest trees. They can move at great speed, with hardly a sound. Sometimes they leap distances of up to 49 feet.

Sluggish sloth

With claws and legs like coat hangers, sloths hang upside down from branches. They also use their long, curved claws to gather leaves and fruits or defend themselves from enemies. Sloths move incredibly slowly, and sleep for up to 18 hours a day.

Extra hand

Many rainforest animals, such as this spider monkey, have a special tail, which curls around branches like a hook. The strong tail grips so well that it works like an extra hand. Spider monkeys can even use their tails to pick leaves and fruits from the trees.

Rainforest plants and trees are a source of many of the world's most important medicines

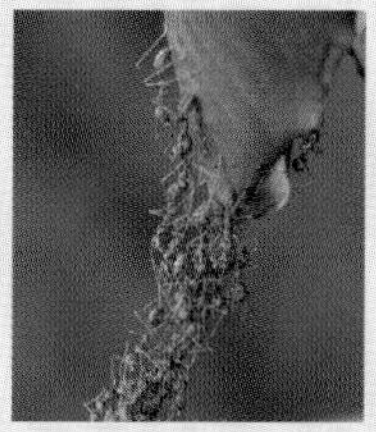

Army ants march in huge armies of over 500,000 ants. They can overpower animals many times larger than themselves

The goliath tarantula is the biggest spider in the world. It would only just fit on a large dinner plate

The tarsier monkey has such huge eyes that one eye can weigh as much as its entire brain

Spiked lizard

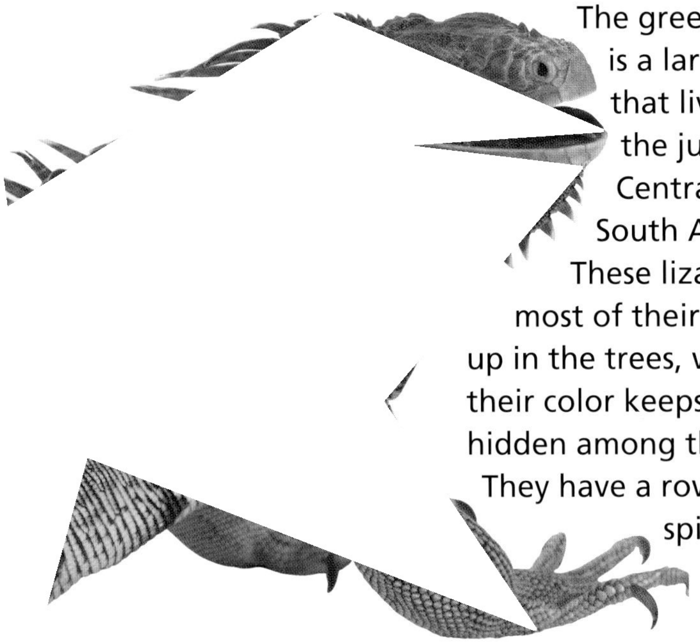

The green iguana is a large lizard that lives in the jungles of Central and South America. These lizards spend most of their time high up in the trees, where their color keeps them hidden among the leaves. They have a row of sharp, spiked scales along their back.

Magical morphos

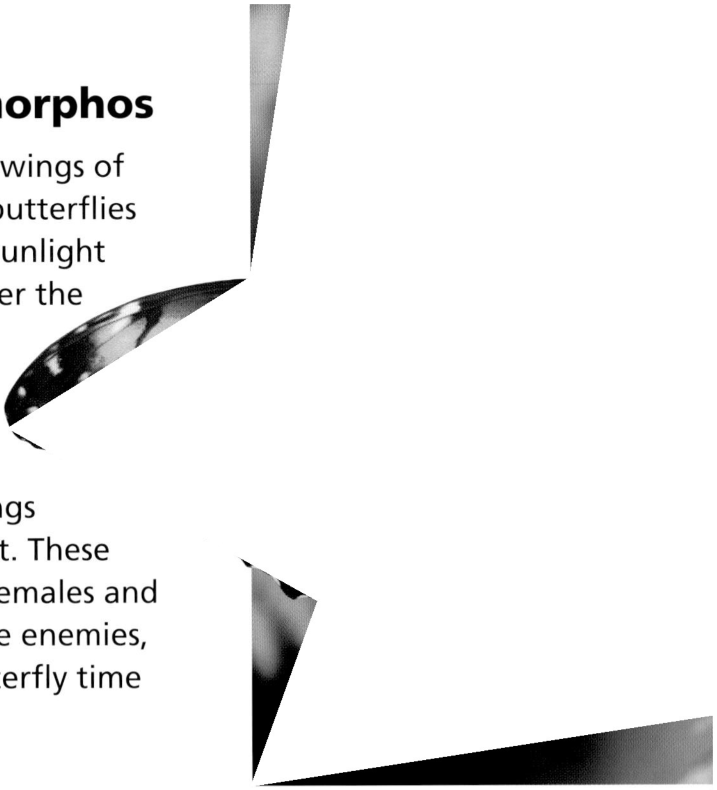

The shiny blue wings of male morpho butterflies sparkle in the sunlight as they soar over the rainforest. The colors are produced by the way the butterflies' wings reflect the light. These wings attract females and may also dazzle enemies, giving the butterfly time to escape.

Big bill

Toucans use their long bills to reach fruits and seeds at the end of thin twigs. The brightly colored bill is hollow inside so it is not as heavy as it looks. Toucans also use their bills to signal to other toucans.

Toucans eat fruit such as papayas

Nutcracker parrot

The strong, hooked bill of the scarlet macaw works like a nutcracker to split open tough forest nuts. Like all parrots, macaws sometimes use one of their feet to hold food up to their mouth.

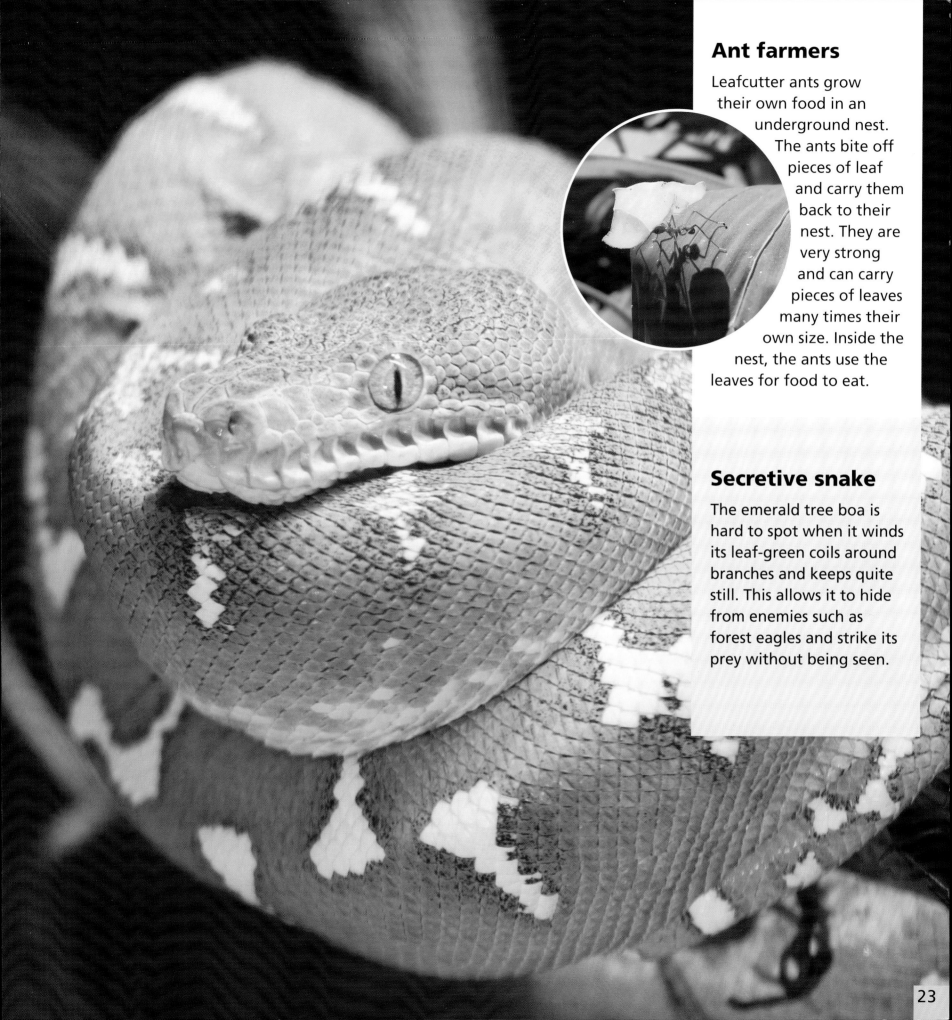

Ant farmers

Leafcutter ants grow their own food in an underground nest. The ants bite off pieces of leaf and carry them back to their nest. They are very strong and can carry pieces of leaves many times their own size. Inside the nest, the ants use the leaves for food to eat.

Secretive snake

The emerald tree boa is hard to spot when it winds its leaf-green coils around branches and keeps quite still. This allows it to hide from enemies such as forest eagles and strike its prey without being seen.

Baby carrier

For the first year of its life a baby orangutan clings to its mother's fur and sleeps in the leafy nest she makes at night. As the baby grows up, its mother teaches it how to make its own nest, where to find food and how to climb and swing from tree to tree in the rainforest.

Big cat

Tigers are the biggest cats in the world. These fierce, strong hunters usually come out at night to catch food, such as deer or wild pigs. Tigers have to work hard for their meals because their prey can run fast or hide behind the forest trees and bushes. Often, a tiger will not catch anything to eat for a week!

Animal armor

Pangolins are covered in overlapping plates, which protect them like a suit of armor. They have no teeth, but use their long tongue to scoop up insects and swallow them whole.

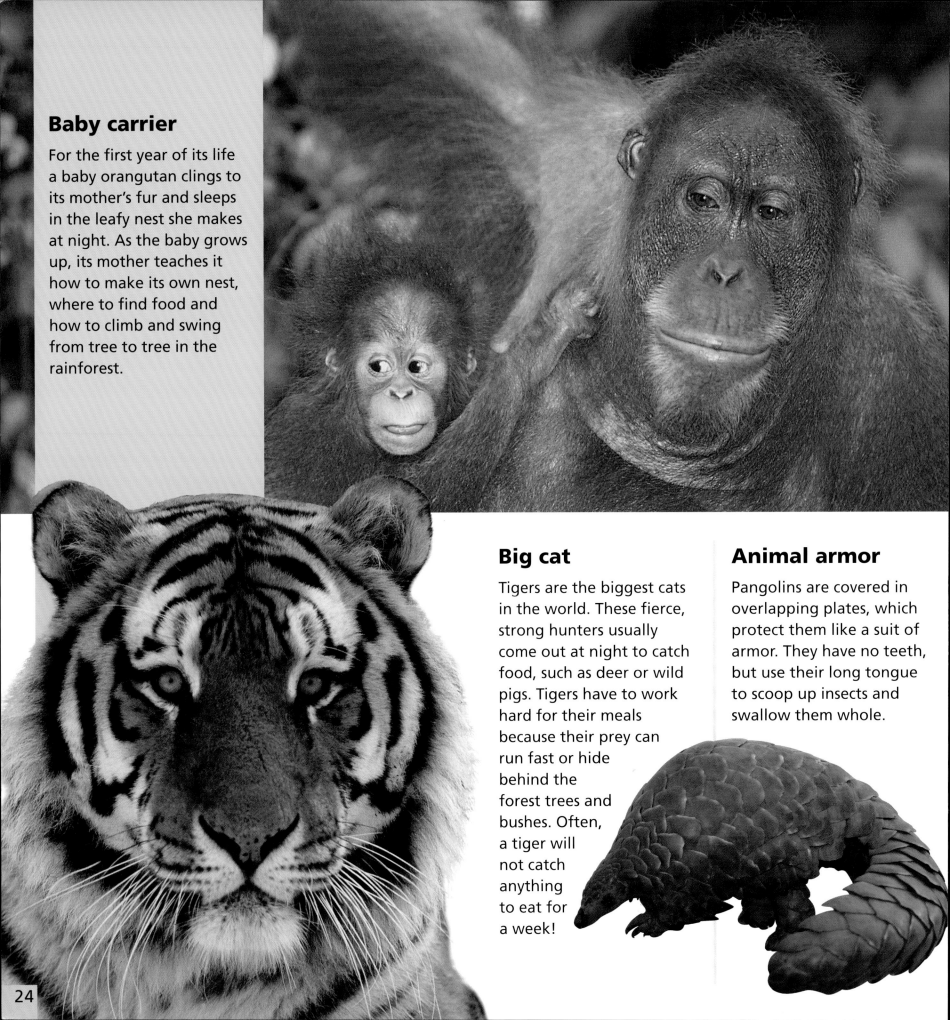

Tree kangaroo

In the rainforests of Australia and New Guinea there are no monkeys and apes. Instead, tree kangaroos climb through the trees, clinging to the branches with the rough, non-slip soles on their feet. The kangaroo's long tail acts as a rudder when it leaps from branch to branch.

Treetop monkeys

Tiny squirrel monkeys leap along thin branches in the rainforest treetops, like the squirrels that live in cooler forests. They live in big groups, sometimes with several hundred monkeys in a group. During the day, they follow their leader through the trees, and at night they sleep huddled together on the branches.

Nosey tapir

The Malayan tapir uses its long nose to pull leaves and fruits from rainforest plants. Its sturdy, rounded body is a good shape for pushing its way through the undergrowth on the rainforest floor. Baby tapirs are well camouflaged from enemies by patterns of stripes and spots.

Bat transport

Fruit bats fly through the forest at night, feeding on flowers and fruits and helping to spread seeds and pollen. The flowers use strong scents to attract the bats, and mostly have pale colors that show up well in the dark.

Face paints

Male mandrills look as if they are wearing face paints! Females prefer males with brightly colored faces. Mandrills live in large groups called troops, with a top male in charge. They search for food on the rainforest floor during the day and climb into the trees to sleep at night.

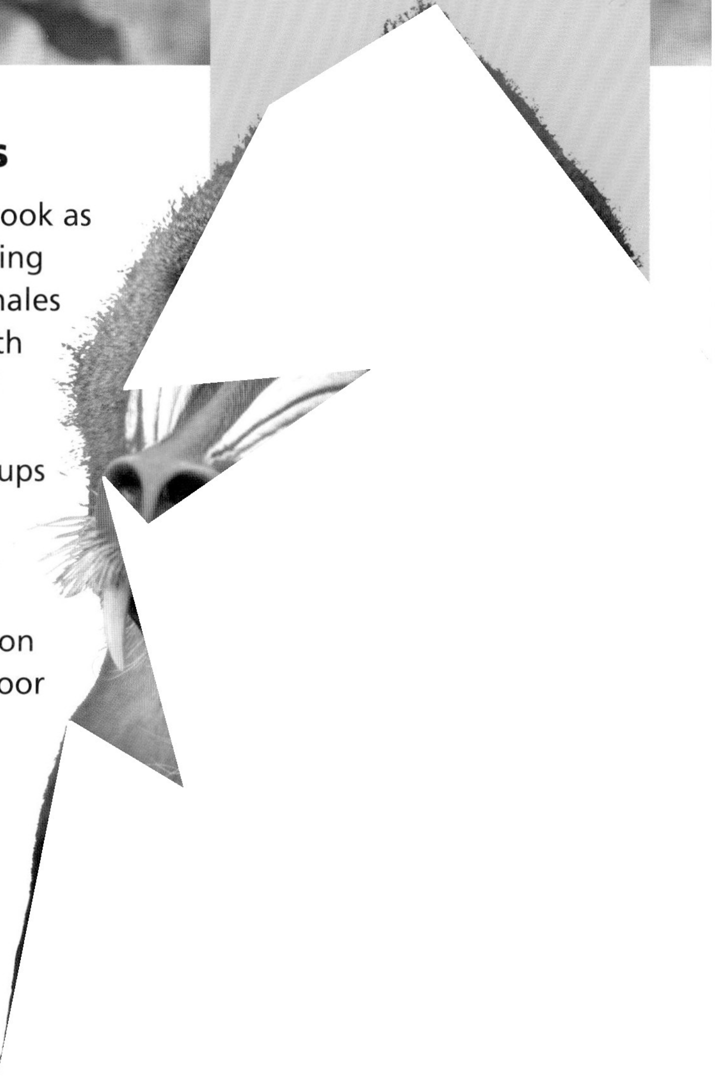

Grasslands

Grasslands grow in places where it is too dry for forests and too wet for deserts. There are two main kinds of grasslands – hot grasslands, such as the African savannah, and warm grasslands, such as the North American prairies, South American pampas grasslands and the Asian steppes.

On the move

To find enough food and water, wildebeest often wander over the grasslands on long journeys called migrations. They may cover thousands of miles each year. Wildebeest are noisy animals and are also called gnus, which is an African word for the loud snort that they sometimes make.

LOCATION

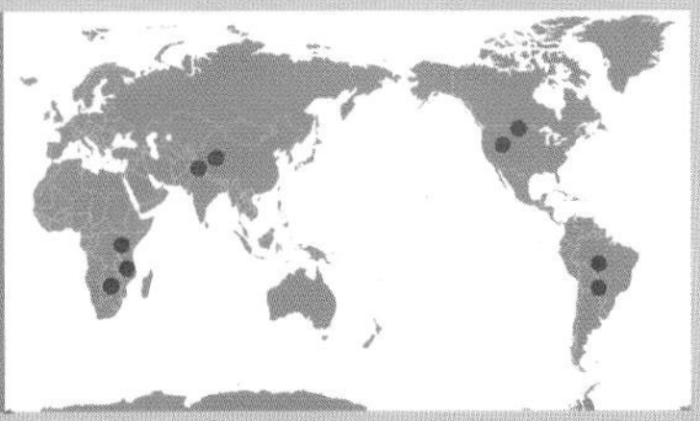

Climate
The prairie grasslands of North America receive between 20 and 35 inches of rainfall in a year

Habitat
Grasses are tough plants. If they are damaged by fire or drought, or eaten by grazing animals, they quickly sprout up again

Earthwatch
Many natural grasslands, such as the prairies, have been turned into farmland for growing crops or grazing farm animals

Hunting cat

Lions live in groups, called prides. The females, called lionesses, catch food and look after the cubs, while males protect the pride. By hunting together, lionesses can kill animals as large as zebras. They are powerful hunters with sharp teeth and claws.

Little and large

A baby elephant, or calf, stays close to its mother and drinks her milk until it is four to six years old. Other adults in an elephant family help too, by shading the calves from the sun and guarding them from predators while they sleep. Calves spend a lot of time playing together too!

Out of the way!

The word rhinoceros means 'horned nose', and rhinos scare their enemies by taking charge at them with these sharp horns. Rhinos have a very thick skin, which protects them from sharp thorns and bites from rivals or enemies. They usually live to around 50 years old.

Olympic sprinter

The cheetah is the fastest animal on land over short distances. It can reach 60 mph in just three seconds! It can only run at top speed for about 60 seconds because it gets too hot. As a cheetah runs, its spiked claws grip the ground like the spikes on a sprinter's running shoes.

Skyscraper neck

A giraffe's extra-long neck allows it to feed on the highest leaves and twigs, up to 20 feet above the ground. Smaller grazing animals, such as zebras and gazelles, cannot reach this food. Giraffes use their long tongue and thick, rubbery lips to strip leaves from branches.

An ostrich's egg is so strong that an adult person can stand on one without breaking it

Elephants eat many different kinds of plants but most of their diet is grass. They feed for about 16 hours a day

A very thirsty adult elephant can drink about 26 gallons of water in five minutes!

The money from tourists watching wildlife on safaris helps to preserve the African grasslands

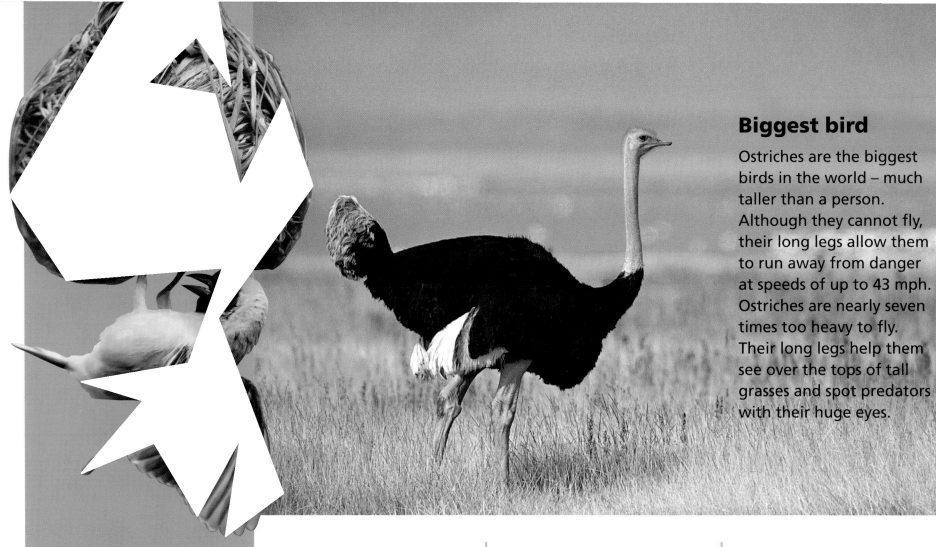

Biggest bird

Ostriches are the biggest birds in the world – much taller than a person. Although they cannot fly, their long legs allow them to run away from danger at speeds of up to 43 mph. Ostriches are nearly seven times too heavy to fly. Their long legs help them see over the tops of tall grasses and spot predators with their huge eyes.

Weaving experts

Male weaverbirds make complex hanging nests by weaving and knotting lots of strips of grass together. Males hang upside down from the finished nest, flicking their wings to attract a female. If the female likes the nest, she lays her eggs inside and raises the young by herself.

Recycling bird

On their long, wide wings, vultures float high in the sky keeping a sharp look out for animal bodies on the ground far below. By feeding on dead animals, vultures clean up the savannah grasslands and recycle the goodness in living things. A bare head and neck allows a vulture to feed without getting its feathers dirty.

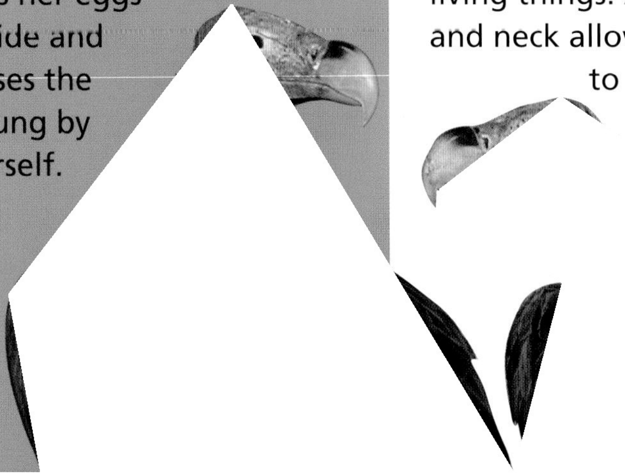

Buzzy bee

As a bumblebee flaps its wings up and down, it makes a buzzing sound. Bumblebees have a hairy body, which keeps them warm. Strong hairs on the bee's back legs form a basket that the bee uses to collect pollen, a yellow dust found in flowers.

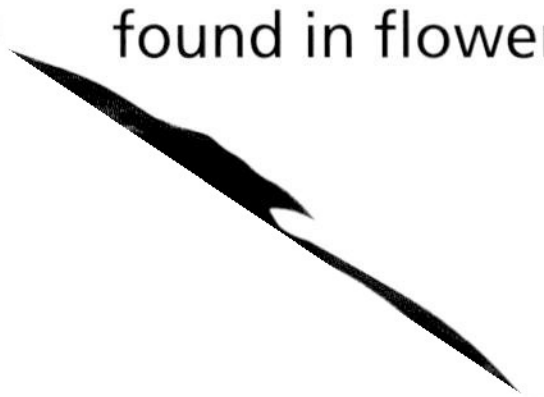

Long jumper

Grasshoppers have very long back legs. The big muscles at the top of these legs give them the power to make very long jumps through the grass. Jumping is quicker than walking, and helps the grasshoppers to escape danger. If a grasshopper is caught by one of its back legs, it can break off the leg to escape from an enemy.

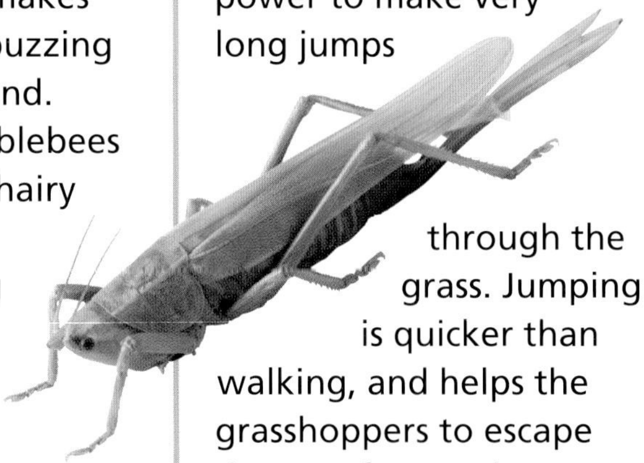

Egg ball

Dung beetles feed on animal droppings, or dung. The adults shape pieces of dung into balls and roll them to a safe place, where they bury them in the ground. The female lays her eggs in the dung ball so the young will have plenty of food to eat when they hatch out of the eggs.

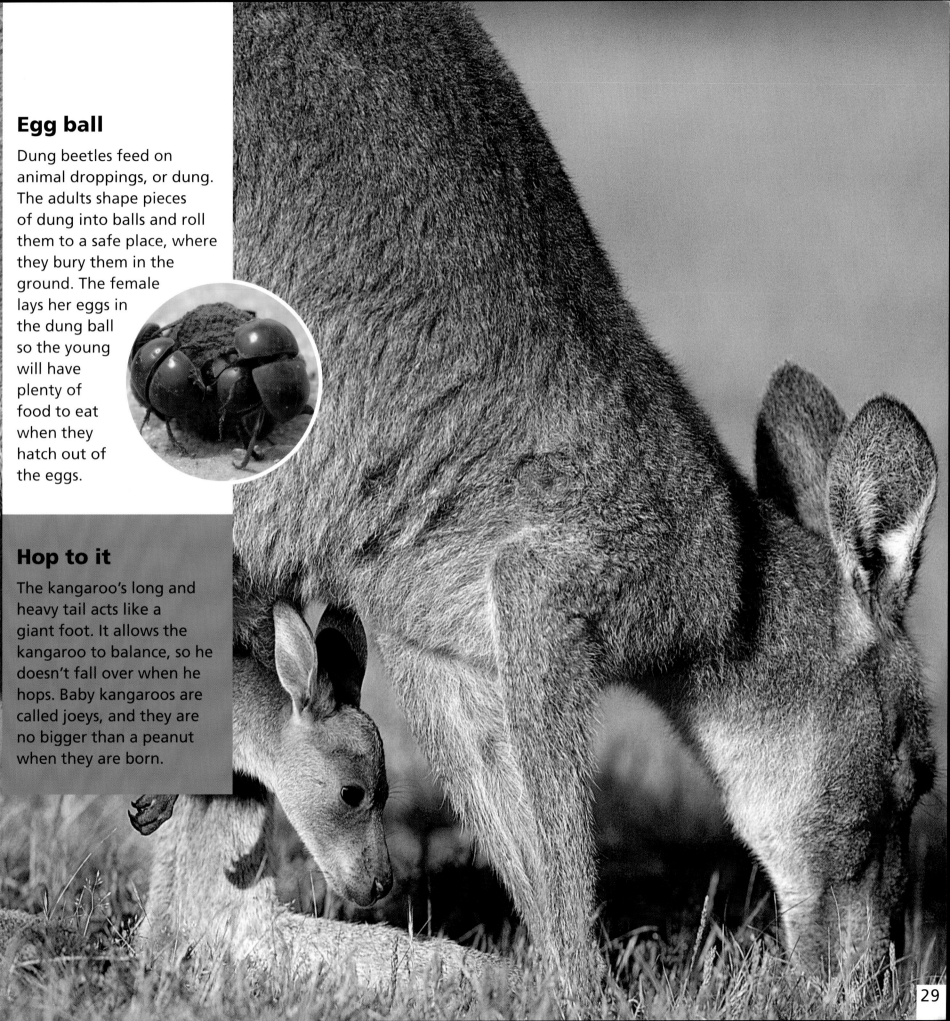

Hop to it

The kangaroo's long and heavy tail acts like a giant foot. It allows the kangaroo to balance, so he doesn't fall over when he hops. Baby kangaroos are called joeys, and they are no bigger than a peanut when they are born.

Deserts

Deserts are very dry places, where it is usually very hot by day and freezing cold at night. There are few large animals in deserts because there is not enough food and water to keep them alive. Smaller animals hide away in burrows during the day and come out at night, when it is cooler and damper.

Big ears

The fennec fox has huge ears, which work like radiators to give off heat and keep it cool. Big ears are also useful for tracking the sounds made by the fox's prey. The long hairs inside a fennec fox's ears keep out all the dust and sand.

Storage hump

A camel's hump is made up mostly of fat, which can be broken down to provide energy when food and water are hard to find. Dromedary camels, from Africa, have one hump, while Bactrian camels, from Asia, have two humps.

A camel can drink up to 13 gallons of water in a few minutes

LOCATION

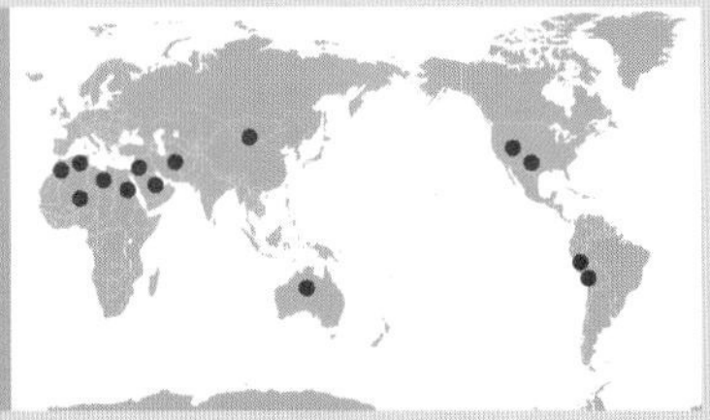

Climate
Deserts are places where there is usually less than 10 inches of rain a year. Some deserts see no rain at all for several years

Habitat
The Sahara Desert covers an area of North Africa almost as big as the USA. It is the largest desert in the world

Earthwatch
Some deserts are getting bigger, which may be linked to climate change or the problems caused by people, or for both reasons

Never thirsty

Kangaroo rats do not drink at all, but get all the moisture they need from their food. They are named after their long back legs, which look like those of a real kangaroo. Kangaroo rats use their long legs to jump out of reach of predators.

Winning races

The wild ass, or onager, can run as fast as a racehorse and goes on long journeys to find enough to eat and drink. It can survive for two or three days without drinking, which means it can survive in dry desert conditions.

Speedy rabbit

The jackrabbit bounds across the desert at speeds of up to 35 mph on its powerful back legs, allowing it to escape from predators. It likes to come out in the cool of the night, and, like the fennec fox, has big ears to give off heat.

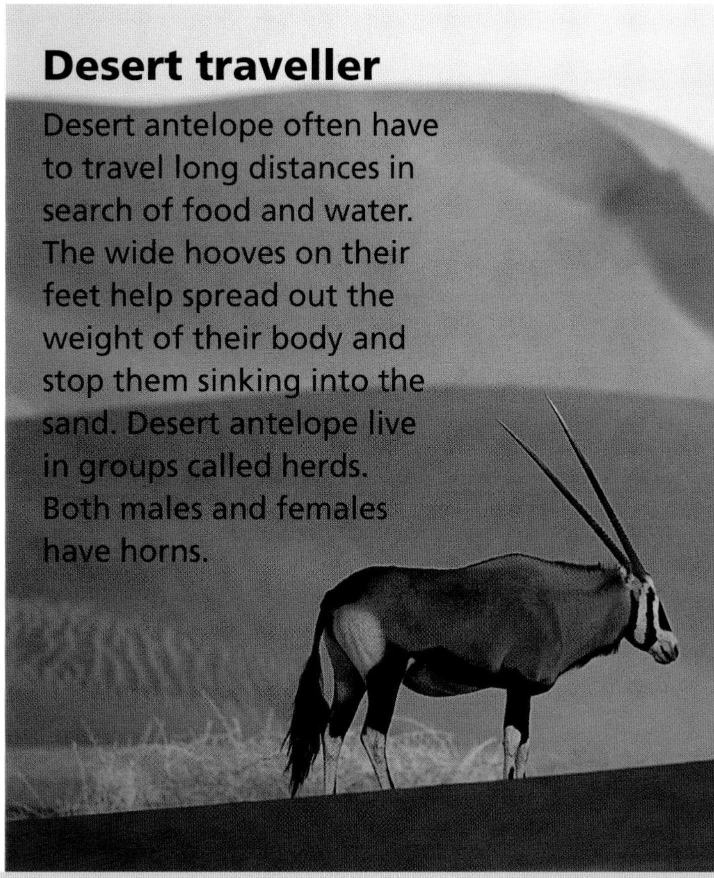

Desert traveller

Desert antelope often have to travel long distances in search of food and water. The wide hooves on their feet help spread out the weight of their body and stop them sinking into the sand. Desert antelope live in groups called herds. Both males and females have horns.

Modern desert towns use large amounts of energy and water, most of which has to be brought in from outside the desert

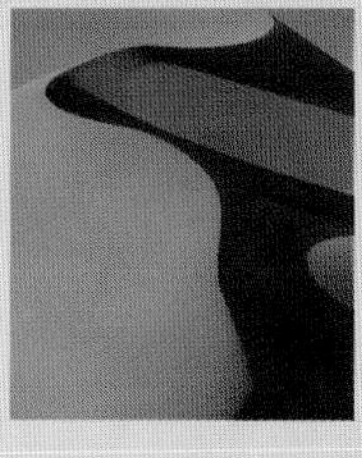

Deserts are not always hot, even in the daytime. It can be as cold as −30°F in Asia's Gobi Desert

Gila ('heela') monsters are endangered, large poisonous lizards that live in the deserts of North America

Only really hardy plants like the cactus can survive in the desert. When it rains, cacti can store loads of water

Honey jars

At rainy times, some honeypot ants store the sweet liquids from plants inside their bodies. They stay underground, and when food is hard to find, other ants feed from these living honeypots.

Shy runner

The roadrunner is a type of cuckoo that is often seen on desert roads. It is a shy bird that runs quickly away from danger at speeds of up to 15 mph. Its long tail works like a brake or a rudder, and helps the bird stop suddenly or swerve in a different direction.

Keep away!

When a rattlesnake shakes the dry scales on its tail this makes a buzzing sound. The buzz tells predators, "Keep away! I have a poisonous bite and am very dangerous." Rattlesnakes use their poison, called venom, to kill their prey at cool times of the day.

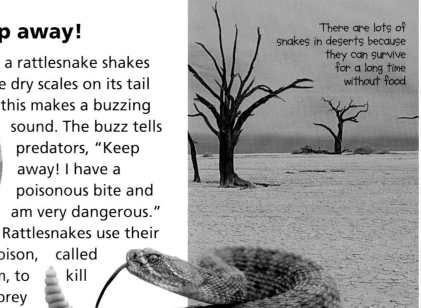

There are lots of snakes in deserts because they can survive for a long time without food

Flying flocks

Parakeets fly over the Australian deserts in large flocks that may contain thousands of birds. These fast-flying parrots fly long distances in search of water. They avoid the hottest part of the day, feeding on seeds in the early morning or late afternoon, when it is cooler.

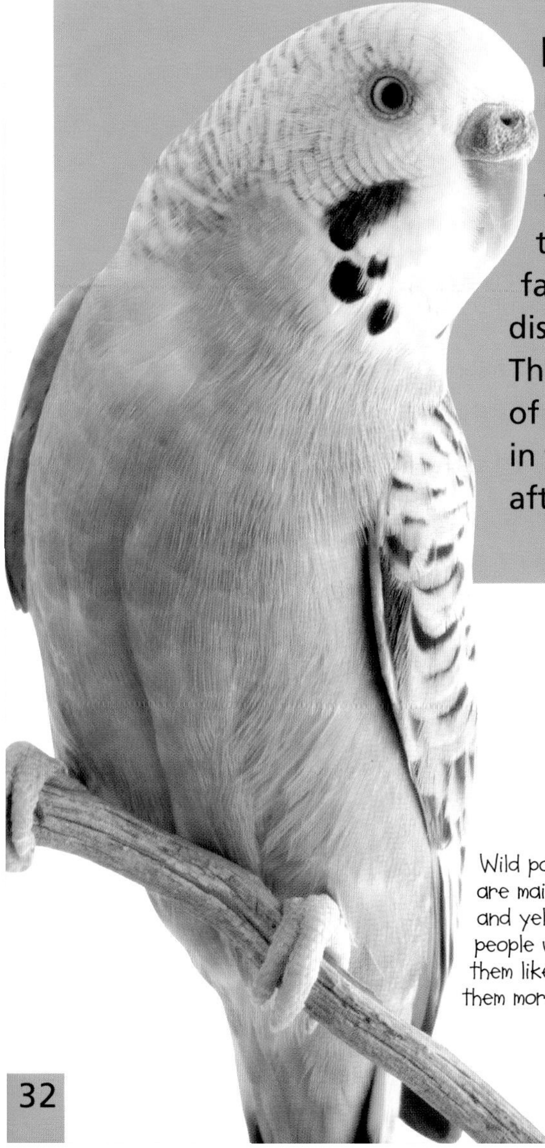

Wild parakeets are mainly green and yellow, but people who breed them like to make them more colorful

Spiny protection

The cactus wren builds a large, dome-shaped nest in the middle of a spiny cactus. The parent wrens have tough feathers and hard, scaly legs, which prevents them from getting scratched on the cactus spines.

Cactus spines protect the baby birds from predators, like a spiked barbed-wire fence

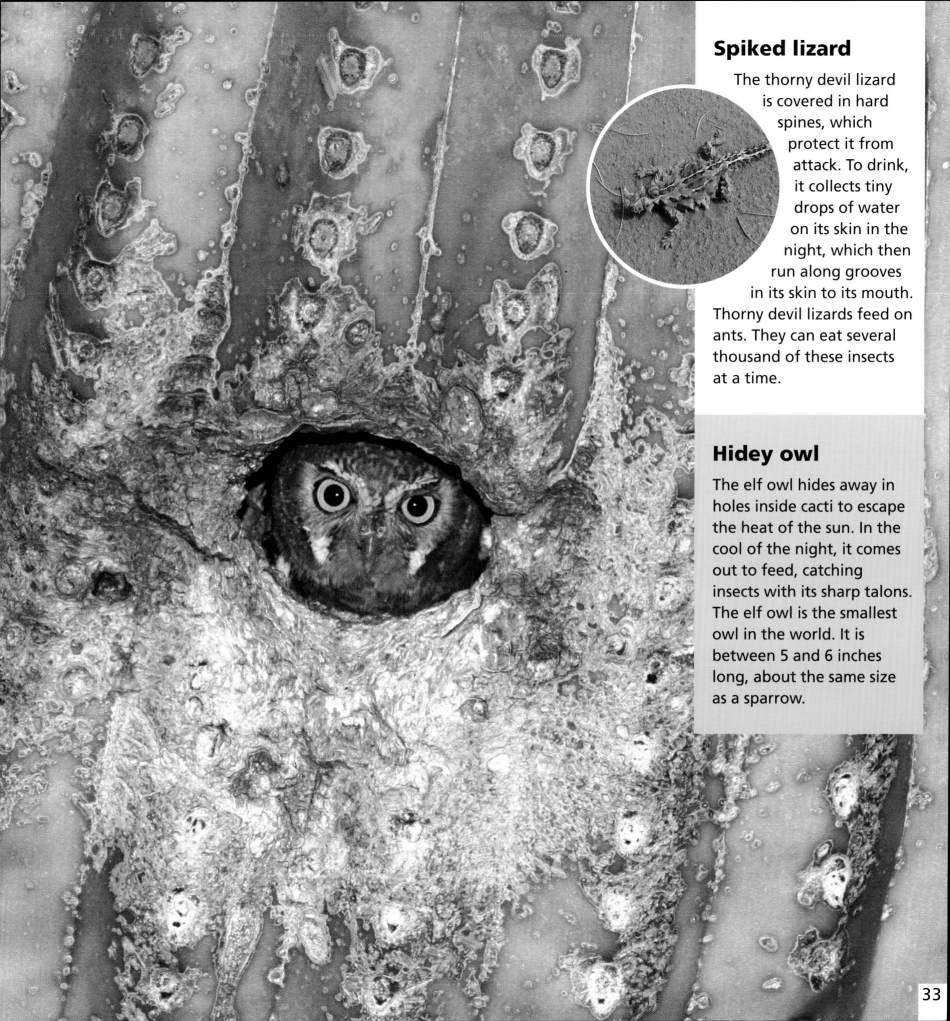

Spiked lizard

The thorny devil lizard is covered in hard spines, which protect it from attack. To drink, it collects tiny drops of water on its skin in the night, which then run along grooves in its skin to its mouth. Thorny devil lizards feed on ants. They can eat several thousand of these insects at a time.

Hidey owl

The elf owl hides away in holes inside cacti to escape the heat of the sun. In the cool of the night, it comes out to feed, catching insects with its sharp talons. The elf owl is the smallest owl in the world. It is between 5 and 6 inches long, about the same size as a sparrow.

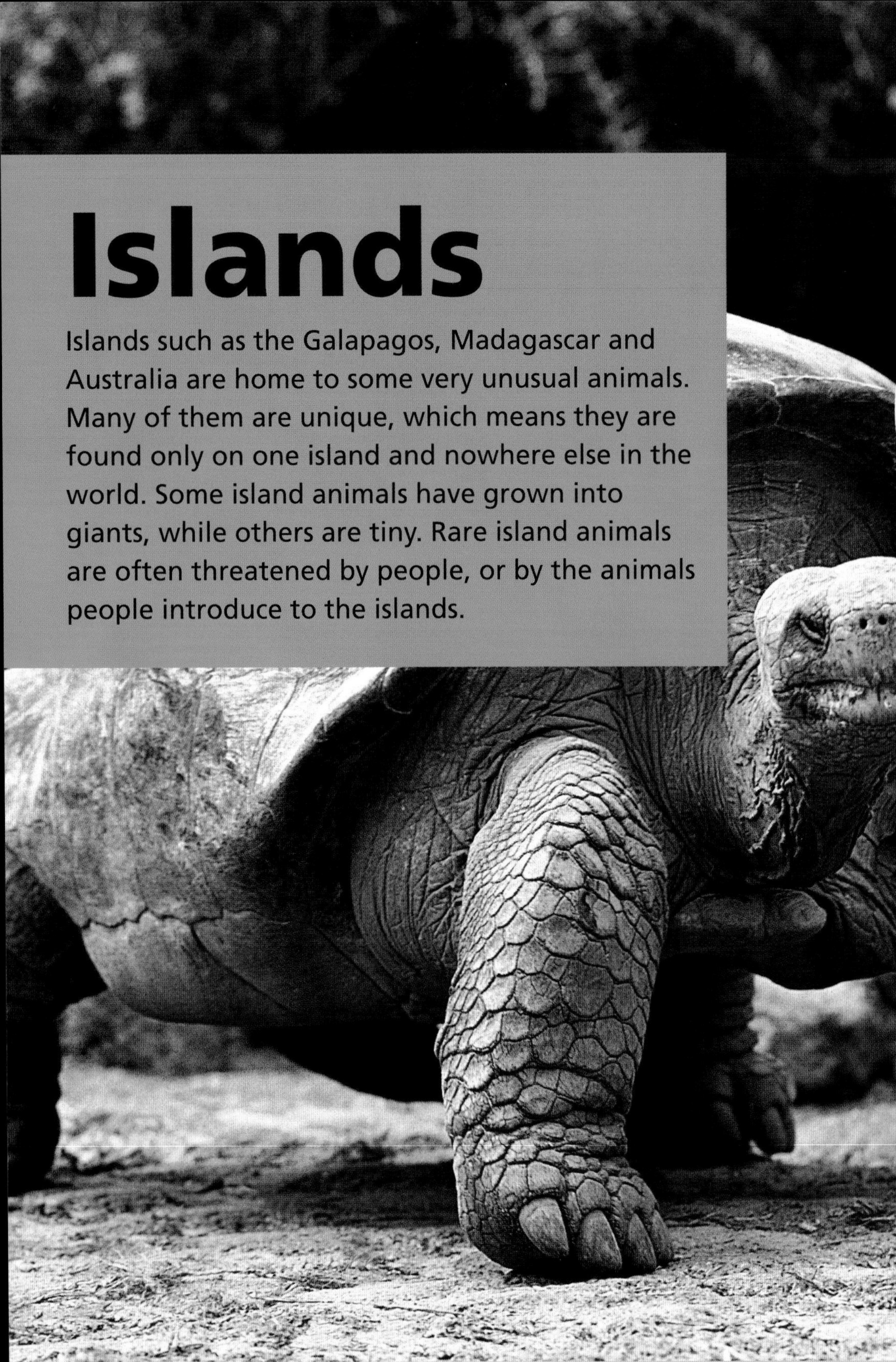

Islands

Islands such as the Galapagos, Madagascar and Australia are home to some very unusual animals. Many of them are unique, which means they are found only on one island and nowhere else in the world. Some island animals have grown into giants, while others are tiny. Rare island animals are often threatened by people, or by the animals people introduce to the islands.

Flightless bird

The kiwi of New Zealand cannot fly, and behaves more like a mammal than a bird. It comes out at night, sniffing for worms and insects with the sensitive nostrils at the end of its long bill. It is rare for a bird to have a good sense of smell.

Island giants

The Galapagos Islands are home to twelve kinds of giant tortoises. The word "Galapagos" is Spanish for a saddle that turns up at the front, like the shells of some of these tortoises. They grow up to 51 inches long and can weigh as much as three men. Giant tortoises may live for over 150 years.

LOCATION

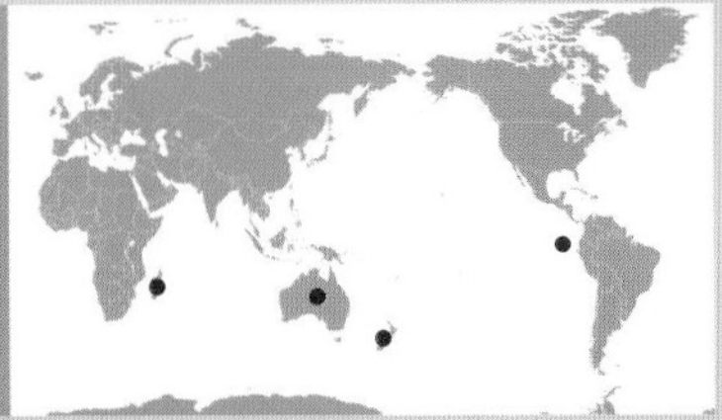

Climate
The Galapagos Islands are on the Equator where it is usually really hot, but cold water currents help keep it cool here

Habitat
Madagascar is the world's fourth largest island. More than 80 per cent of the plants and animals on the island are unique

Earthwatch
Since European settlers arrived in Australia about 200 years ago, they have cleared many forests

Big nose

The male proboscis monkey from the island of Borneo has a very large nose, which probably helps him attract females. Females have much smaller noses. Proboscis monkeys are very agile. They leap through mangrove trees, using their long tails to help them balance.

Baby pouch

Australia is home to many different mammals that rear their babies in pouches on the mother's body. A baby koala lives in its mother's pouch for six months until it is big and strong enough to be carried around on her back.

Alarm clock bird

Kookaburras are sometimes called the "bushman's clock" because their loud chuckling call wakes people up in the Australian bush at dawn. Kookaburras are giant kingfishers, but rarely eat fish. Instead, they catch snakes, small mammals and other birds.

Striped tail

The ring-tailed lemur's striped tail helps it balance. The male ring-tails rub their tails with scent from the glands on their bodies, and have "stink fights" with other males! Lifting their tails in the air signals to other lemurs.

Dreadful dragon

The Komodo dragon is the largest lizard in the world, growing up to 10 feet long. Although it is not a fire-breathing dragon, it is still a very dangerous reptile. It kills water buffalo with its sharp claws and a bite full of deadly bacteria.

The tuataras that live on islands off the coast of New Zealand look similar to their relatives that lived with the dinosaurs

The leaves of the eucalyptus trees that koalas eat do not give them much energy, so they spend most of their time asleep

Two-thirds of the world's chameleons live on the island of Madagascar. Lemurs and birds called vangas live here too

The marine iguana of the Galapagos Islands is the only lizard that swims and feeds in the sea. It holds its breath underwater

Coral reefs

Coral reefs are like the rainforests of the sea because they are full of such a variety of wildlife. They grow mainly in the shallow, clear water of tropical oceans where the coral animals have enough sunlight and warmth to survive. The warm waters are full of brightly colored fish, sponges, sea anemones, worms, starfish and sea snakes.

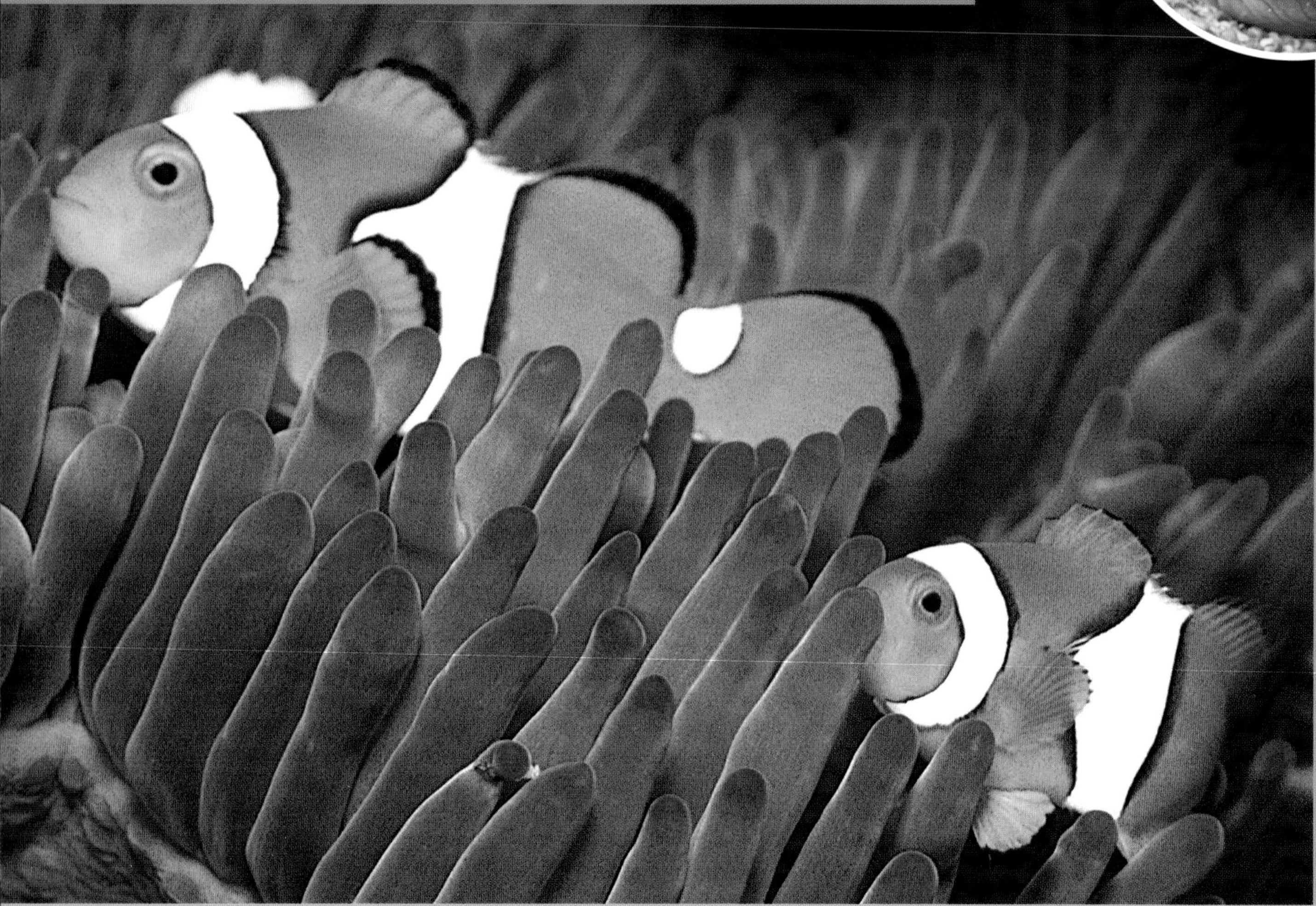

Razor teeth

Moray eels hide in gaps between the coral, darting out to catch fish that swim nearby. They have long, razor-sharp teeth to grab their prey. Unlike most other moray eels, zebra moray eels have flat teeth for crushing the hard bodies of crabs, sea urchins and other prey.

Help each other

Many coral reef animals help each other survive by feeding or protecting each other. The clown fish keeps safe by hiding among the stinging tentacles of sea anemones. It covers itself in slime for protection against the stings. The bright colors of the fish may warn predators of the anemones' dangerous tentacles, and therefore help keep both animals safe.

LOCATION

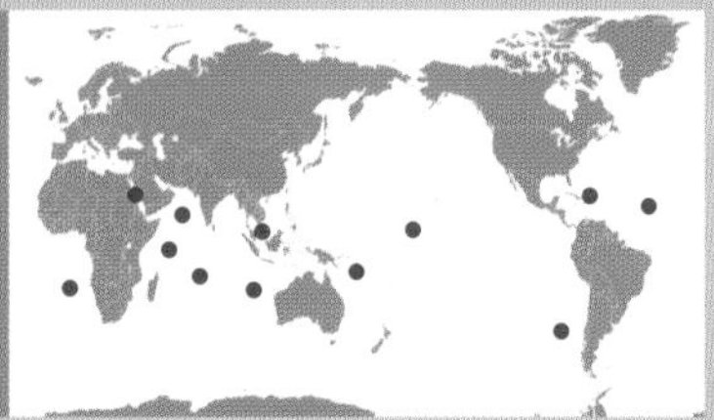

Climate

Coral reefs are very sensitive to changes in water temperature, and they take thousands of years to form

Habitat

A coral reef is made up of billions of little coral skeletons, piled on top of each other. Most are no bigger than your thumbnail

Earthwatch

Coral reefs are threatened by pollution, overfishing, drilling for oil and by the dumping of waste on top of the reef

Plant or animal?

Corals look rather like flowers, but they are really tiny animals related to sea anemones and jellyfish. Each coral animal, called a polyp, has a soft body and a ring of tentacles that wave in the water to trap particles of food. It grows a protective casing around its soft body. When the coral animals die, their empty casings build up to form a reef, on which new corals grow.

How many arms?

Do you know how many arms an octopus has? These arms are lined with suckers and are used for swimming, gripping prey and fighting. Octopuses have large eyes to help them find their prey, and sharp, beak-like jaws to bite and tear their food. They can change color for camouflage, or as their mood changes.

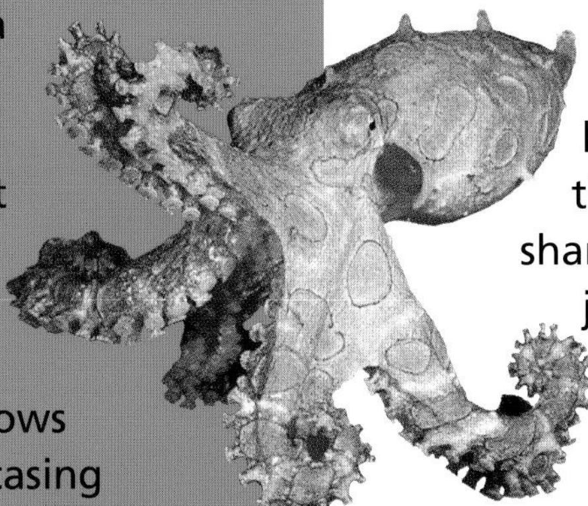

Fish with a beak

Parrotfish have strong jaws that look rather like a parrot's beak. They use their strong 'beak' to scrape off little plants that are growing on the coral. Male parrotfish are more brightly colored than the females.

Inflatable fish

If a porcupine fish is threatened, it quickly gulps down water or air, puffing up its body so it is too big for most predators to swallow. When the fish inflates its body, spines stick out of its skin, rather like the spiny quills of a porcupine.

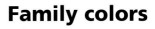

Family colors

The bright colors and patterns of butterfly fish help them recognize other fish like themselves and attract a mate. Their long snouts help them reach into small holes in the reef to find food.

The Great Barrier Reef stretches for nearly 1,250 miles off Australia. The biggest in the world, it can be seen from the Moon!

The lionfish is covered in lots of long, highly poisonous spines, which give would-be predators a very nasty sting

The largest predators on a coral reef are reef sharks, which patrol the deep water by the reef, looking for stray fish

The weedy sea dragon looks more like a piece of seaweed than a fish! Fleshy flaps cover its body, camouflaging it well

Oceans

Animals live at different levels in the oceans, from the sunlit waters on the surface to the darkest depths. Ocean temperatures are less extreme than on land, and the water supports the animals' bodies. Shoreline animals have to cope with dramatic change every day, because the seawater moves up and down the beach twice a day with the tides, and the waves also crash against the shore.

Stone tools

Sea otters crack open shellfish and sea urchins by bashing them against a stone. Then the otter is able to eat the soft flesh inside. Sea otters have thick, waterproof fur to keep them warm. An adult sea otter has hundreds of millions of hairs.

What's different?

True seals, such as gray seals, swim with their back flippers, while sea lions swim with their front flippers. Sea lions are better at moving on land than true seals. They can use their front flippers to push their bodies up off the ground, and turn their back flippers forwards to work like feet.

LOCATION

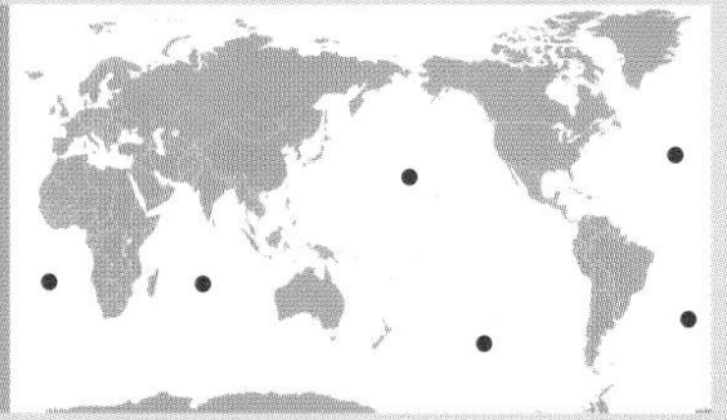

Climate
The wind creates strong currents on the ocean's surface, and these have an effect on the weather around the world

Habitat
The world has five oceans – the Pacific, Atlantic, Indian, Southern and Arctic Oceans. They are all linked together

Earthwatch
Many whales have been hunted almost to extinction. Controlling the hunting helps, but many are still threatened

Ocean giant

Humpback whales strain fish and small floating creatures from the seawater using fringed plates that hang down from their jaws like curtains. They have to come to the surface to breathe. They breathe by using a pair of blowholes on the top of their head.

Streamlined shape

A dolphin's body is a good shape for slipping easily through the water. It also has a smooth skin, with no hairs to slow it down while it swims. To move forwards, dolphins beat their tail flukes up and down. Their fins help them steer and change direction.

Fish holder

Puffins catch small fish underwater. They can hold twelve or more fish in their bill at once. Sharp edges to the bill and spines on the tongue stop the fish from sliding out. The puffin also uses its bill to dig a nesting burrow in a grassy cliff top.

Clever camouflage

An oystercatcher's eggs look like pebbles, so they are difficult for predators to spot on a pebbly beach. The male and female take turns sitting on the eggs, which hatch after about four weeks. The fluffy chicks can run around soon after hatching.

Washing line

A cormorant's feathers are not waterproof, unlike the feathers of most other waterbirds. After swimming underwater to catch fish, a cormorant holds out its wings to dry them. It pushes itself through the water with its webbed feet, reaching depths of about 33 feet.

Feed me

A herring gull chick pecks at a red spot on its parent's bill to make the parent cough up food. Herring gulls feed on fish out at sea and swallow the food to help them carry it for long distances. Herring gulls feed on rubbish dumps as well as out at sea.

Starfish usually have five arms, but may have between four and fifty arms!

Manta rays grow to 23 feet across, and weigh over 1.5 tons. They sometimes leap out of the water to escape predators

A female hawksbill turtle can lay over 250 eggs at one time! The eggs then take about 60 days to hatch

Sperm whales can stay underwater for more than two hours, hunting for giant squid and other prey

Baby beaches

Sea turtles, such as green turtles, spend most of their lives swimming through the oceans with their strong flippers. The females come ashore at night to lay their eggs on sandy beaches. Each female green turtle lays about 100 eggs at a time. She has to lay many eggs because most of her babies will not survive.

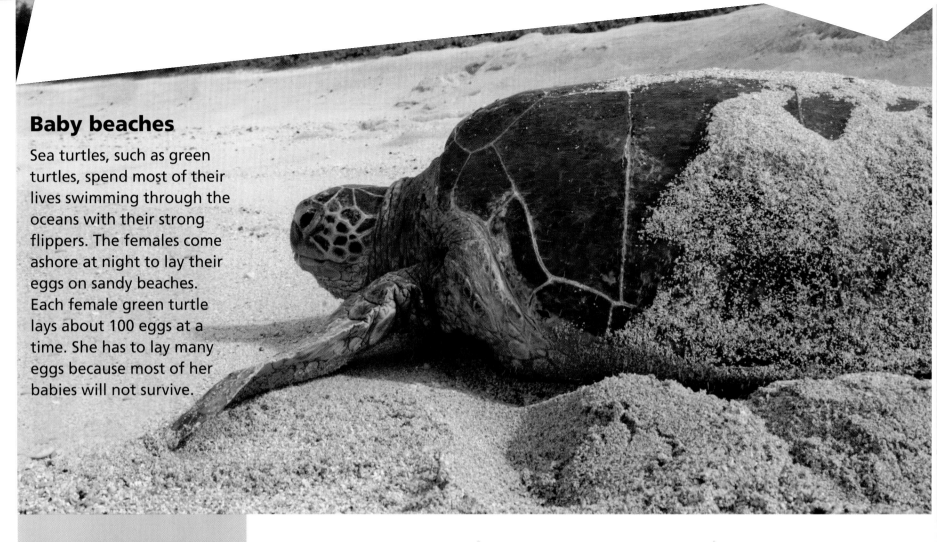

Borrowed home

Unlike most crabs, a hermit crab does not have a hard shell on the back part of its body. So, it borrows an empty shell to live in. The crab can hide inside the shell if it is attacked by a predator, such as a seabird. As it grows bigger, it swaps the shell for a larger one.

Plant or animal?

A sea anemone looks rather like a flower, but it is in fact an animal. It catches fish and other small sea creatures in its stinging tentacles. When the tide goes out, it pulls in its tentacles and fills its body with water so it looks like a blob of jelly. This stops it from drying out until the tide comes in and covers it with water again.

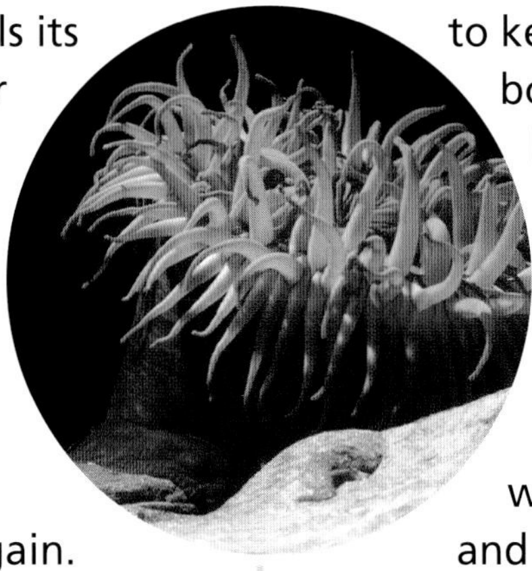

New arms for old

If one of a starfish's arms is damaged or bitten off, it can grow a new one.

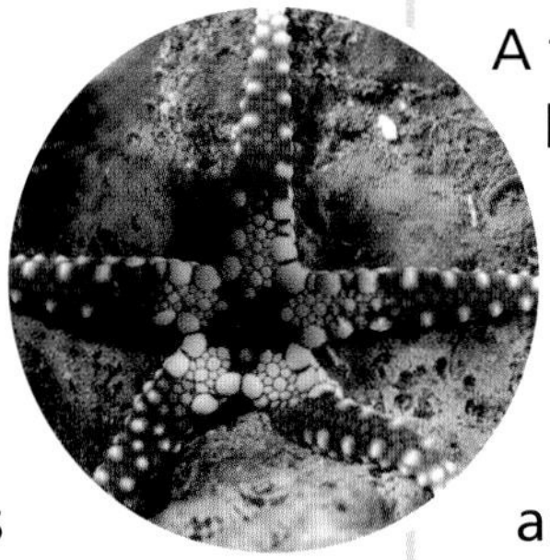

A starfish has to keep its body damp. At low tide, when the beach dries out, it hides underwater in rock pools or under rocks, where it is cool and moist.

Pouched horse

A female seahorse lays her eggs in a pouch on the front of the male's body. The male seahorse carries the developing babies around for a few weeks until they are ready to swim off and look after themselves. The baby seahorses suck up thousands of shrimp a day, and grow quickly.

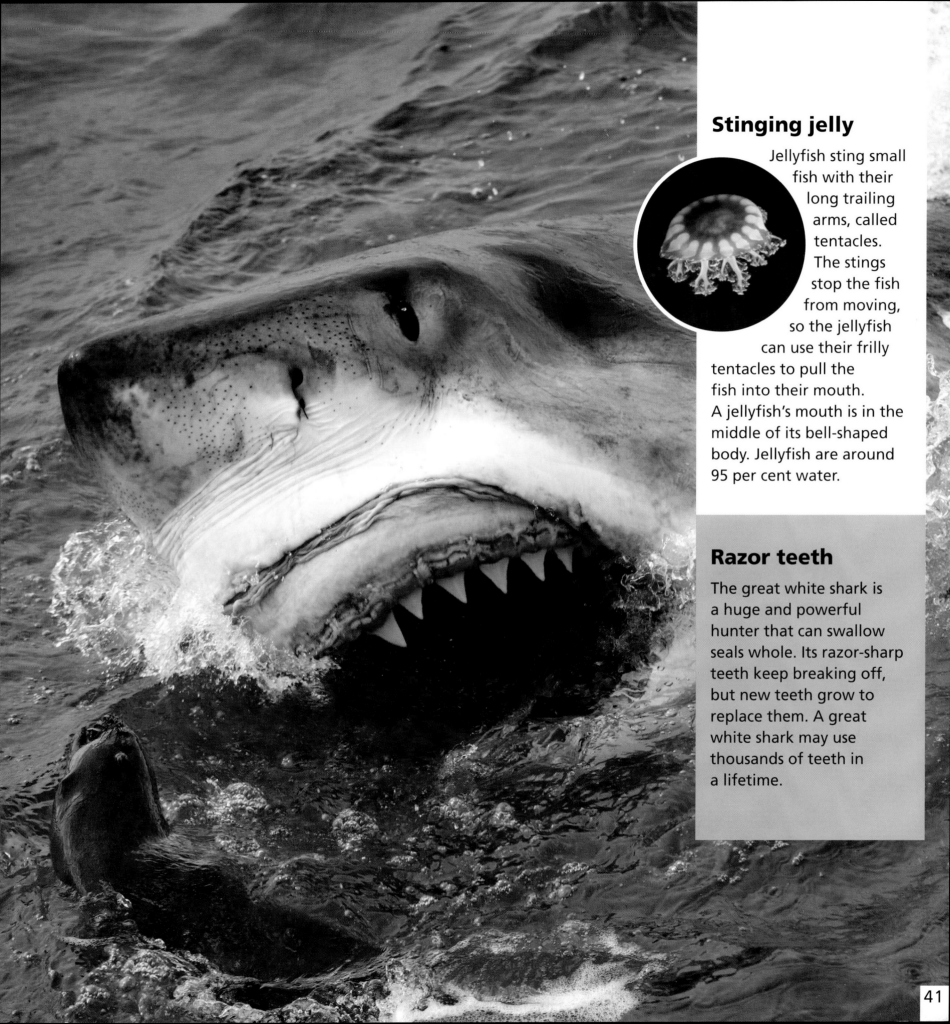

Stinging jelly

Jellyfish sting small fish with their long trailing arms, called tentacles. The stings stop the fish from moving, so the jellyfish can use their frilly tentacles to pull the fish into their mouth. A jellyfish's mouth is in the middle of its bell-shaped body. Jellyfish are around 95 per cent water.

Razor teeth

The great white shark is a huge and powerful hunter that can swallow seals whole. Its razor-sharp teeth keep breaking off, but new teeth grow to replace them. A great white shark may use thousands of teeth in a lifetime.

Polar areas

In the frozen lands and oceans around the North Pole and the South Pole, animals have to survive bitterly cold temperatures, fierce winds and long, dark winters. Polar animals rely on thick fur, feathers or layers of fat to keep them warm. Many animals journey to polar regions for the short, warm summers, when there is plenty of food to eat and lots of safe nesting places.

Perfect penguins

Penguins cannot fly, but they are brilliant swimmers. They use their flippers to 'fly' underwater, and spend up to three-quarters of their lives in the sea. They come to land only to nest and rear their young. Large numbers of penguins nest together in huge, noisy colonies of as many as a million birds.

LOCATION

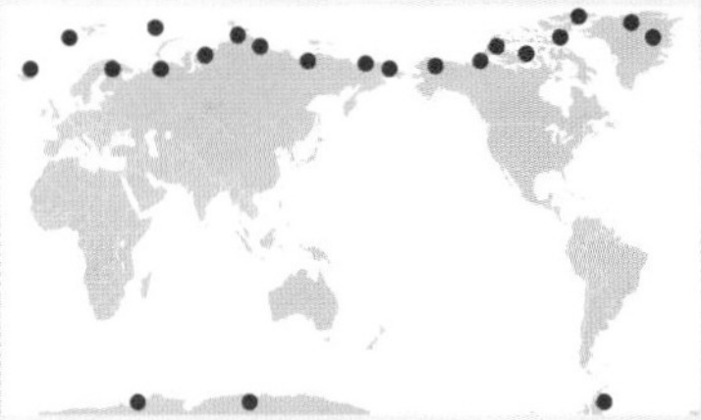

Climate
The average winter temperature in Antarctica is –76°F. Winds of up to 186 mph cause severe blizzards and snowdrifts

Habitat
Antarctica is a vast frozen continent around the South Pole. It is one and a half times the size of the USA

Earthwatch
Some of the ice is melting in polar areas because of 'global warming,' or an increase in the Earth's average temperature

Summer bird

Every year, Arctic terns fly from one end of the world to the other and back again. This means they have one summer near the North Pole and then a second summer near the South Pole. They never have to survive cold winter weather and always have plenty of food and daylight.

Longest wings

The wandering albatross has the largest wingspan of any bird. It glides over the cold oceans in the southern part of the globe searching for food, and comes to land only to nest. Chicks stay in the nest for nearly a year, using their thick feathers and layers of fat to keep warm.

Great white bear

Polar bear cubs are born in a warm den, which their mother digs under the snow. The cubs are tiny and helpless at first, but they grow quickly as they feed on her rich milk. In just one year, the cubs are as big as a person. They stay with their mother for about two years while she teaches them how to hunt and survive.

Musical marks

Adult harp seals have black markings, which are shaped like a harp. Their pups are born on sheets of ice floating on the ocean, and have thick, fluffy white coats to keep them warm. The white color also helps them blend into a background of white ice, making it harder for predators to spot them.

Helpful whales

Killer whales hunt in large groups called pods. This helps them catch larger prey than one whale could catch on its own. Killer whales catch seals and other large whales as well as fish and seabirds, including penguins.

Walrus warmth

Walruses have very thick layers of fat under their skin, which keep them warm in freezing oceans near the North Pole. Both males and females have long, pointed teeth called tusks, which they may use to fight each other, or for defense. Walruses use their fleshy noses and whiskers to feel for food on the seabed.

Most of Antarctica is covered by a sheet of ice, which in some places is as much as 2.5 miles deep

Male emperor penguins do not eat for over 15 weeks while they keep an egg warm and wait for their chick to hatch

The icefish has a chemical in its blood that stops it freezing, like antifreeze stops water freezing in a car radiator

Polar areas are called 'Lands of the Midnight Sun' because in the summer it never gets dark and the Sun can shine all night

Summer vacation

Snow geese fly thousands of miles to spend the summer in cold northern regions. There they can nest and raise their young in places where there are few predators to disturb them. The snow geese have thick, fluffy feathers next to their skin to keep them warm in the freezing conditions.

Feather duvet

The female eider duck pulls out some of her own fluffy feathers to line her nest. This lining works like a feather duvet. It traps warm air near the eggs so they develop properly. The feathers also help hide the eggs from predators, such as foxes and gulls.

Distance runner

Wolverines hunt alone at night, chasing their prey for many miles without getting tired. These animals are very strong for their size and have a powerful bite. They can kill animals as big as reindeer.

Snowshoe feet

Arctic hares have big, furry feet, which allow them to move over the snow without sinking in very far. To escape from predators such as Arctic foxes, they can run very fast on their extra-long back legs.

Changing color

The Arctic fox grows brown fur in summer and white fur in winter. This means that it always blends in with the background, and can creep up on its prey without being seen. It wraps its thick bushy tail around its body like a furry blanket to keep itself warm.

Polar ghost

Gliding silently over the ground, snowy owls swoop down to catch prey in their sharp talons. Snowy owls nest in a shallow dip in the ground, lined with moss or feathers. They do not lay all their eggs at once, so there is a mix of ages and sizes of chicks in their nest at the same time.

Christmas deer

Reindeer, or caribou, are the only deer in which both males and females grow antlers. Reindeer make long journeys north in the summer and then south again in the winter. The calves are born during the journey, and can run faster than a person when they are only one day old. They have to keep up with the adults to stay safe from predators.

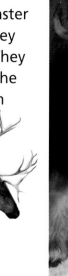

Long hair

Musk oxen have very long fur coats to help them keep warm. The edges of their hooves are sharp enough to dig through snow and ice and reach food hidden underneath. If a group of musk oxen are attacked, they form a tight circle with the young in the middle. The adults defend the young with their big, curved horns.

Our habitat

Some wild animals live in our homes and yards because there is plenty of food all year round and a variety of places to shelter and nest. During the winter, they may also move to our towns and cities where the weather is warmer than it is in the countryside. Many people also keep them as pets or farm animals.

Keeping bees

People build artificial nests, called hives, for honeybees to use. They can then harvest some of the wax that the bees produce to build their nest. Bees make honey from sweet flower nectar and store this in their nest to help them survive the winter. Beekeepers also take some of this honey for people to eat.

In some cities, there are as many rats as people! They live under our feet in sewers, drains and other underground tunnels

People first started to keep dogs as pets about 12,000 years ago. Cats only became pets about 4,000 years ago

In some European towns, white storks nest on chimneys instead of tall trees. They are believed to bring good fortune

Over 100 years ago, a small flock of starlings were released in New York. Today, there are over 50 million in North America

to learn about animals. Any type of pet needs a lot of daily care and attention.

Keeping cows

Farmers keep cows mainly for their meat and milk, although leather can also be made from their skins. Cow horns can be used to make music or sound warnings, or made into things such as walking sticks, buttons and combs.

Milk is a good source of calcium. This helps our bones grow

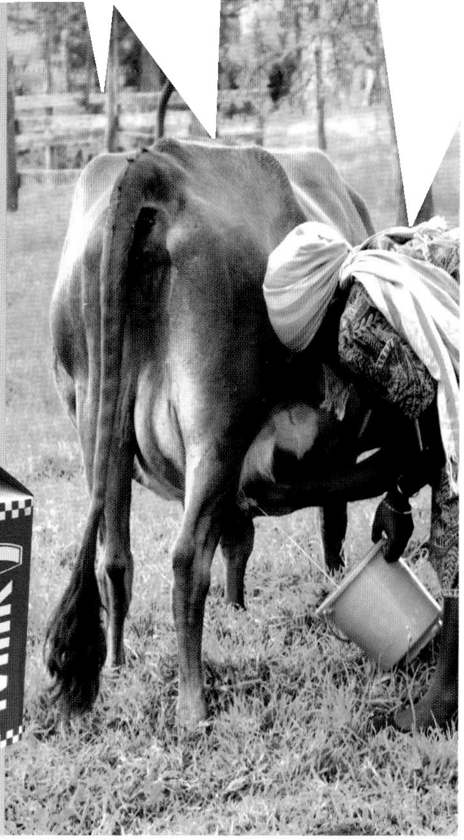

Warning colors

Ladybugs are easy to spot in gardens and parks because of their bright red color. This bright color warns predators that ladybugs taste nasty, so they leave them alone. These much-loved insects are useful to people because they eat the greenflies that damage crops and garden plants. One ladybug can eat up to 50 greenflies a day.

Helpful horses

For thousands of years, people have tamed wild horses and used them for carrying loads, farming, racing and riding. Today, there are hundreds of different kinds of tame horses, from tiny Shetland ponies to huge shire horses. It is essential to groom a horse to keep its coat clean and in good condition.

Woolly fleeces

Most of our wool comes from the woolly coat that sheep grow, which is called a fleece. A sheep's fleece is cut off in spring or summer when the sheep does not need its thick woollen coat to keep warm. This is kind of like getting a haircut. It does not hurt the sheep, and the fleece soon grows back.

Butterfly plants

Plants that produce plenty of sweet nectar encourage butterflies, such as this peacock butterfly, to visit a garden. These plants include polyanthus, catmint, buddleia and honesty. Butterflies find buddleia bushes so attractive that they are called butterfly bushes.

In Australian cities, possums sometimes set up home in the attics of houses

In tropical countries, geckos are welcome in houses because they catch insects. Geckos have suction pads on their toes

About one million dust mites live in a single bed. They feed on the bits of dead skin that flake off our bodies

The world's fastest racehorses are able to run at up to 40 mph over short distances

Town pigeons

Pigeons nest on rocks and cliffs in the wild, and are quite at home nesting on the artificial cliffs provided by the buildings in our towns and cities. People have kept pigeons for eating, for flying in races and for carrying messages tied to their feet.

Rascal raccoons

Like the red fox, the streetwise raccoon will eat almost anything. It thrives in towns and cities in North America, nesting in chimneys or drains instead of the hollow tree trunks it uses in the wild. In a city, a raccoon is safer from traps and hunters, which are a threat in the countryside.

House sparrows

These familiar birds are good at living near people, and have spread to most parts of the world. They usually stay close to buildings, often making their grassy nests in holes in walls. Female sparrows lay four or five eggs, which hatch in about two weeks. The young sparrows are ready to fly from the nest in about another two weeks.

Make it snappy

Alligators have lived in the wetlands of the US state of Florida for hundreds of years. The human population is growing in this area, and the number of alligator attacks on people, pets and farm animals in Florida has increased significantly since the year 2000.

Alligator warning street sign

Motorway hunter

Kestrels often hover above the grassy edges of motorways, looking for mice and other prey moving through the grass below. They beat their wings very fast and spread out their tail to stay in one spot in the air for a long time. When the kestrel spots a meal, it slowly swoops down, grabbing the prey in its sharp claws.

Mouth sponge

Houseflies do not have a mouth with teeth, and can only digest liquid foods. To eat, first they spit onto their food to turn it into a sort of soup. Then they mop this up with the spongy pad on their head. A housefly also has rather unusual feet. They are able to taste its food!

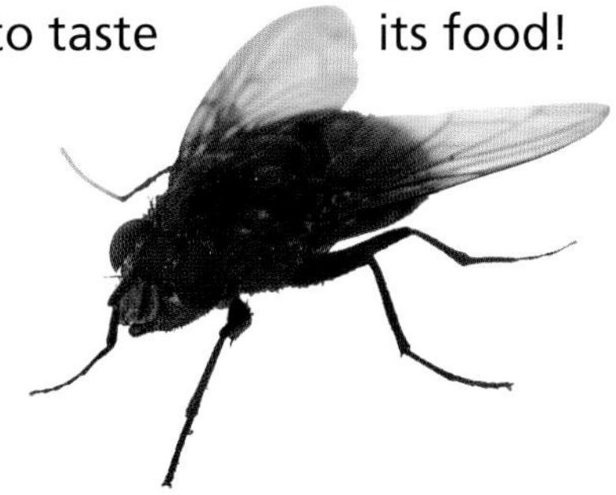

Top dog

Red foxes are members of the dog family, and are common in many cities in Europe, Australia and North America. They are not fussy about where they live or what they eat, often feeding on leftover scraps of food from our rubbish bins. Many foxes live in the countryside, and often commute into towns at night to find food.

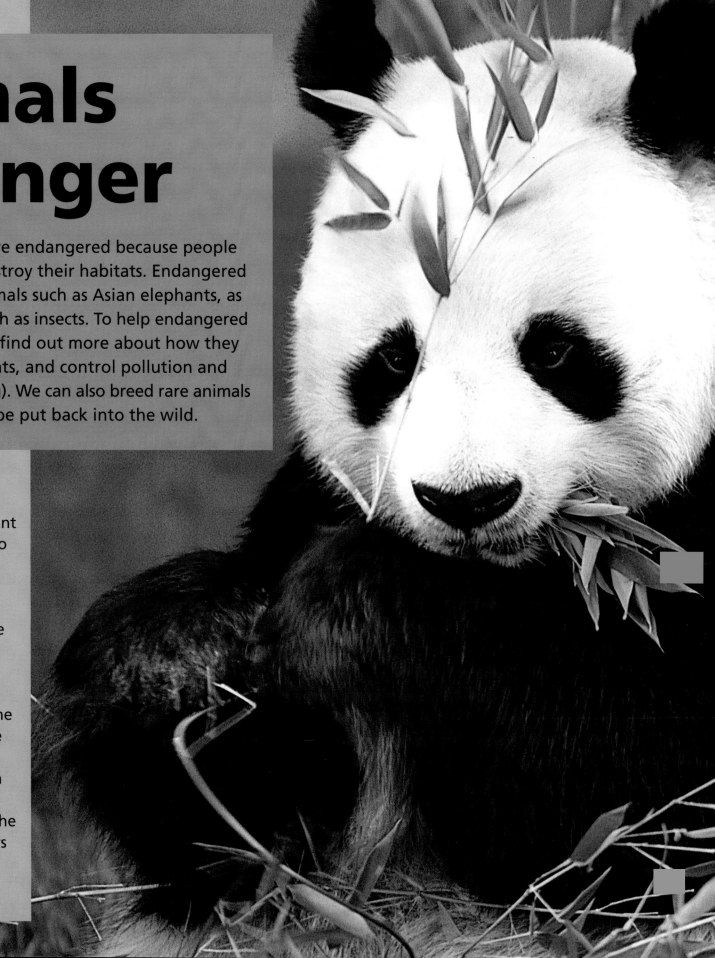

Animals in danger

Thousands of animals are endangered because people hunt or sell them, or destroy their habitats. Endangered animals include big animals such as Asian elephants, as well as small animals such as insects. To help endangered animals survive, we can find out more about how they live, protect their habitats, and control pollution and poaching (illegal hunting). We can also breed rare animals in captivity so they can be put back into the wild.

Night senses

There are about 1,600 giant pandas left in the bamboo forests and mountains of China, where they are protected in nature reserves. At present, these reserves are cut off from each other, but attempts are being made to link them. This would allow the pandas to move from one forest to another. Many pandas have been bred in captivity, and some have been released back into the wild to boost the numbers of pandas living there.

Mountain gorilla

There are only around 650 mountain gorillas left in the wild – in two separate areas of central Africa. Cutting down trees for farmland and timber is a threat to gorillas for two reasons. Firstly, it means that they are losing their habitat. Also, with the forests opened up, hunters are able to kill them more easily. One way to protect mountain gorillas is to let tourists pay to watch and photograph them. This money can then be used to protect them from hunters. Unfortunately, wars in the region make this difficult.

Golden lion tamarin

Named for the bright orange mane around their faces, less than 100 golden lion tamarins were left in 1980 in the forests of Brazil. 98 per cent of their forest home had been destroyed, and many were captured for zoos. Conservation of the remaining forest, and putting some captive-bred tamarins back into the wild has rescued them from extinction.

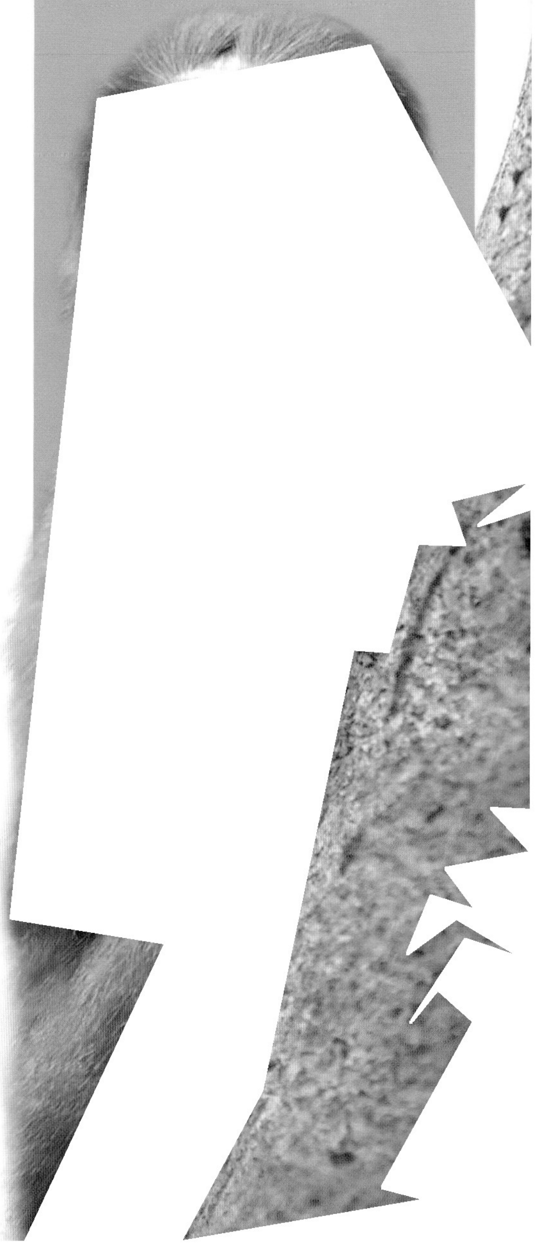

Asian elephant

Asian elephants are in much greater danger than their African cousins. There are probably only between 28,000 and 44,000 Asian elephants left in the wild. These elephants are threatened by the growing numbers of people who farm the land where they once lived undisturbed.

Snow leopard

No one is sure how many snow leopards survive in the wild, because they live high in the mountains of central Asia and are very difficult to count and study. The main threat to their survival is farming. Herds of sheep and goats overgraze the mountain grasslands, leaving less food for the wild sheep – the snow leopard's main prey.

Bactrian camel

The two-humped Bactrian camel has thick, dark fur, which keeps it warm in the cold deserts of Asia. Fewer than 1,000 of these camels survive in the wild. This is due to hunting and pollution, and is also because their habitat is being destroyed by mining and gas pipe laying. Two nature reserves have been set up to protect them.

Tiger

Over the last 100 years, tiger numbers have fallen drastically. The South China tiger is the most endangered tiger. There are only around 30 of these animals left. All tigers are threatened by people who poach for their body parts, such as their bones, skin and internal organs. These parts are used in some traditional medicines. Cutting down plants also damages their habitat.

Hyacinth macaw

The deep blue hyacinth macaw is the largest kind of macaw, which is a type of parrot. Thousands of these stunning birds have been captured and sold as pets. To capture them, people cut down trees to remove the young macaws from their nest holes. This destroys the nest site for future generations, and also destroys their habitat. The illegal trade in pet macaws must be controlled, their habitats protected, and birds bred in captivity released into the wild.

Yangtze River dolphin

The rarest of all the whales, dolphins and porpoises, it is more than likely that the Yangtze River dolphin is now extinct. There were once thousands of these unusual dolphins living in the Yangtze River in China, but scientists could not find any in 2006. They have been affected by pollution, the noise from boats, and over-fishing.

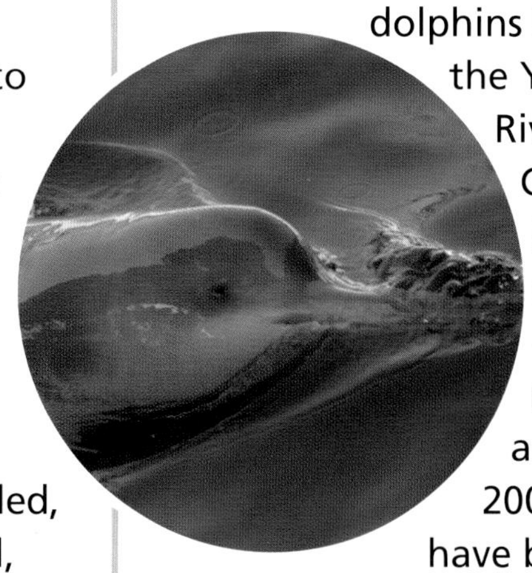

Leatherback turtle

The leatherback turtle is the biggest turtle alive today, and it is critically endangered. In some places, nesting females are killed for their meat, and their eggs are taken for food. Out at sea, the adult turtles often get trapped in fishing gear. This means they are unable to swim to the surface to breathe, and they drown under the water. Patrolling beaches helps prevent poaching, and can allow baby turtles to reach the sea safely.

Blue whale

Blue whales were killed in huge numbers in the first half of the twentieth century, and their bodies were used to make oil. They were hunted almost to extinction until 1966, when hunting was banned all over the world. Once, there could have been up to 350,000 blue whales swimming in the oceans.

Black rhino

In the early twentieth century, there were about 100,000 black rhinos living over most of Africa. Now there are only about 2,700. Their horns are made into dagger handles, and are ground up for use in traditional Asian medicines. Today, most black rhinos only manage to survive in south and east Africa in nature reserves, where they are protected by armed guards.

Amazing animals

From the biggest animal in the world to one that can paralyze ten people with its poison, these four pages are stuffed full of amazing facts about animals that break all sorts of records. You'll find out some incredible things about their weird diets, special senses, extraordinary eggs, as well as how they survive in extreme habitats.

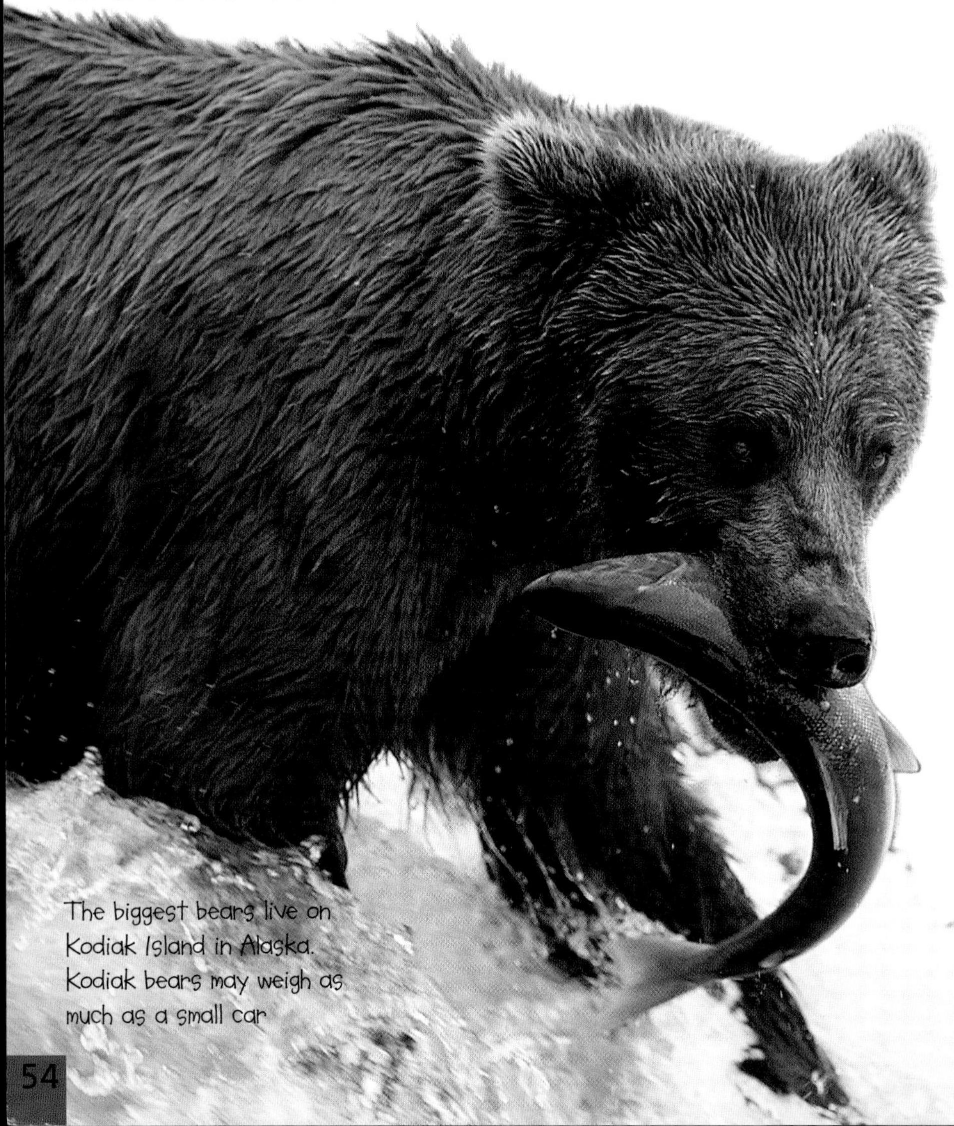

The biggest bears live on Kodiak Island in Alaska. Kodiak bears may weigh as much as a small car

Size

The adult female blue whale is the largest animal in the world. The seawater supports her huge body, which can reach over 98 feet long, and can weigh more than 150 tons.

FACT The biggest fish are the whale shark and the basking shark. They grow up to 39 feet long, and feed on tiny plankton in the sea

FACT The goliath beetle is the heaviest insect. It weighs up to 3.5 ounces – that is nearly as heavy as an apple!

FACT The smallest bird in the world is the bee hummingbird, at only 2 inches long. Bee hummingbirds have the fewest feathers of all birds

FACT The giraffe is the tallest animal in the world. Its neck grows up to 8 feet long. Giraffes can weigh as much as 3,000 pounds

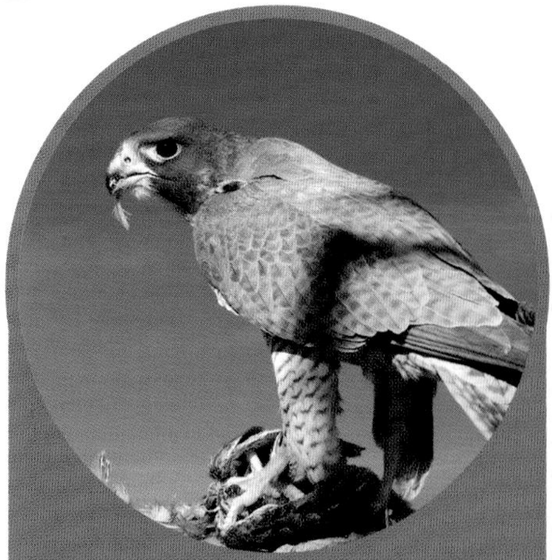

Speed

The fastest animal in the world is the peregrine falcon. To catch its prey, first it soars to a great height, then it drops very steeply through the air at super speeds of up to 124 mph.

FACT An ostrich can cover up to 110 yards in just five seconds. That's about twice as quick as the fastest human sprinter!

FACT The three-toed sloth is the slowest mammal, moving along the ground at speeds of only about 6 feet a minute

FACT The fastest fish in the sea is the sailfish. It can zoom through the water at speeds of over 60 mph

FACT Dragonflies can fly at over 18 mph. Amazingly, they can also hover, go backwards and forwards, and come to an instant stop

Senses

Sharks have an excellent sense of smell. They can detect the scent of blood from injured prey up to 1,640 feet away. They also have very sharp hearing, and these two senses combined make them ferocious hunters!

FACT Most spiders have eight eyes, but their eyesight is poor. They rely mainly on scent and vibrations to find out about their surroundings

FACT The male emperor moth can smell the special courtship scents that female emperor moths give off from around 7 miles away

FACT Some long-eared bats have ears almost as long as their bodies. These help them detect tiny midges up to 65.5 feet away

FACT A bird's eyes are often as big as its brain. An ostrich's eyes are bigger than its brain. Ostriches have the largest eyes of any bird

Defense

The front horn of a white rhino can grow to be twice as long as a person's arm. Amazingly, it is made of hairs packed really tightly together – there's no bone in the middle of the horn.

FACT The front claws of a Kodiak brown bear can grow as long as a person's hand. The bears use these claws mainly for digging

FACT Caribou reindeer have really big antlers. They can grow to be more than 60 inches long

FACT Some butterflies and moths hide from predators by looking like leaves, twigs or even bird droppings

FACT Bombardier beetles squirt a boiling hot spray of poisonous chemicals at their attackers. They can spray this in any direction they wish

Survival

In order to survive extremely cold winters, marmots (also known as prairie dogs) hibernate in their burrows for as long as 10 months.

FACT Some mice can survive in meat cold-stores, where the temperature can sometimes fall below 16°F

FACT Camels don't sweat until their bodies reach 104°F. When they find water, they can drink 22 gallons in just 10 minutes!

FACT In the desert, the male sand grouse flies up to 50 miles in search of water. He carries the water back to his chicks in his chest feathers

FACT The highest living mammals are the yaks of the Himalayas. They climb as high as 20,000 feet, and endure temperatures of −40°F

Poisonous

Nearly all spiders use poison to kill or paralyze their prey, or to defend themselves. The Brazilian wandering spider has poison strong enough to kill 225 mice. Its bite has killed several people.

FACT One blue-ringed octopus can paralyze up to ten people with its poison. It has bright blue rings on its body to warn that it is deadly

FACT Only female wasps are able to sting. This is because the sting is made from the egg-laying tube, which only females have

FACT Giant centipedes with poisonous claws live in the American rainforests. These centipedes can grow up to 12 inches long

FACT Less than a quarter of all snakes are poisonous. The most poisonous snake in the world is the black-headed sea snake

Wings and limbs

The Australian sugar glider has flaps of skin along the sides of its body, which work like wings. The sugar glider can glide for more than 164 feet when moving between trees.

FACT A hummingbird beats its wings up to 75 times a second. It is this amazingly fast wing beating that produces the humming sound

FACT The male quetzal is a shiny green bird from Central America. His tail is more than twice the length of his body, and helps him attract a mate

FACT The African jacana has the longest toes of any bird. They help spread out its weight, so it is able to walk across swampy ground

FACT The wandering albatross has the biggest wingspan of any bird. It measures more than 10 feet from one wingtip to the other

Teeth and beaks

An elephant's tusks act as its front teeth. They grow at a rate of around 7 inches a year. A male's tusks can weigh up to 132 pounds. Elephant tusks are made of a hard material called ivory.

FACT The longest fangs of any snake belong to the gaboon viper. These can grow up to almost 2 inches long

FACT The Australian pelican has the longest bill in the world. Male pelican bills can grow up to 18.5 inches long

FACT The wrybill of New Zealand is the only bird with a bill that curves to the right rather than to the left, but no one knows why this is!

FACT The hawfinch has the most powerful bill of any bird. It can easily crack cherry stones with this bill

Eggs and nests

Some tiny insects called termites build huge mud towers. These can be over 26 feet high. It takes termites between 10 and 20 years to build these incredible homes, and each home shelters millions of termites.

FACT The female gray partridge lays the most eggs at one time of any bird. She can lay up to 20!

FACT Only a few mammals, such as the platypus and the spiny anteater, lay eggs instead of giving birth to babies

FACT The biggest birds' nest is built by the bald eagle. One nest can weigh as much as 4,400 pounds – about the same as two army jeeps

FACT The nests of African sociable weaver birds look like the thatched roof of a cottage. As many as 300 birds can live in one nest

Babies

A newborn baby elephant weighs more than an adult human. Baby elephants feed on their mother's milk for up to six years. A female elephant has a really long pregnancy, lasting for 22 months.

FACT A baby blue whale weighs about 2.5 tons when it is born. That's hundreds of times heavier than a human baby weighs at birth

FACT Mother crocodiles carry their babies in their mouth to take them from their nest to the water. They can carry up to 20 babies at a time

FACT Anacondas give birth to live young, instead of laying eggs. The newborn anacondas are only 2.3 inches long, but can grow up to be over 20 feet!

FACT When it is born, a baby kangaroo, called a joey, is so small that it would fit into a teaspoon!

Food

Giant anteaters mainly eat ants and termites. Their tongues are about 2 feet long, and they use this long, sticky tongue to lick up as many as 30,000 of these tiny insects a day.

FACT An egg-eating snake can unhinge its jaws. This allows it to swallow eggs twice the size of its own head!

FACT Vampire bats are the only mammals that feed just on blood. They lap up blood from their prey, rather than sucking it

FACT Saltwater crocodiles can catch and kill really big animals like zebras and cattle. They can survive up to two years between meals

FACT A chameleon can stick out its long tongue to almost twice the length of its body. It catches insects on the tongue's swollen, sticky tip

Lifespan

The lifespan of an animal is the length of time for which it lives. Some animals live much longer than humans, while others have really short lives. Generally, the larger an animal is, the longer it tends to live.

Arctic clam – 220 years
Giant tortoise – over 200 years
Crocodile – up to 100 years
Killer whale – 90 years
Elephant – up to 70 years
Parrot – 50–80 years
Whale shark – 60 years
American lobster – 50 years
Hippopotamus – 45 years
Tiger – 22 years
Goldfish – 10–25 years
Goat – 15 years
Fox – 14 years
Platypus – 10 years
Toucan – 6 years
Rabbit – 6–8 years
Hamster – 3–4 years
Common shrew – 1 year
Housefly – 2–4 weeks
Mayfly – 3 hours

A baby gorilla is not strong enough to walk by itself until it is at least two and a half years old. It rides on its mother's back until then

Glossary

Acid rain
A type of rain that is formed when certain gases are released into the air and mix with water vapor. Acid rain damages trees and kills fish when it gets into rivers and lakes.

Camouflage
Features or patterns that make plants and animals look like their surroundings. Camouflage is useful because it allows plants and animals to hide from their enemies.

Captivity
When an animal is not free to roam wild, but is kept by people in a zoo or some other place that it is unable to leave of its own accord.

Colony
A group of animals belonging to the same **species**, that live together in a group. Many birds, for example penguins, live together in colonies.

Coniferous
A type of tree with thin leaves that produces cones, for example, pine trees. Coniferous trees are usually **evergreen**.

Continent
One of the main areas of land on Earth. There are seven continents in total. These are Europe, Asia, Africa, North America, South America, Australia and Antarctica.

Coral reef
A structure in the sea made up of the skeletons of tiny sea animals called polyps. Over many years a coral reef builds up as old polyps die and new ones grow on top of them.

Current
Currents are moving streams of sea water both on and below the surface. On the sea's surface they are caused by the wind. Currents affect weather systems around the world.

Deciduous
A type of tree that sheds its leaves each year in the fall. Most trees are deciduous. If a tree is not deciduous it is called **evergreen**.

Drought
A long period of dry weather, when very little, or no, rain falls. This makes it hard for crops to survive.

Endangered
To be threatened by something. An endangered animal is usually an animal threatened by **extinction**. Endangered animals are often kept in **captivity**.

Environment
The environment is a word used to describe everything that surrounds us on Earth. Earth's environment is unique. It is made up of air, water, and the heat and light from the Sun. Sometimes when people talk about the environment they are referring to the condition of the Earth, and to problems such as **global warming**.

Evergreen
A type of tree that does not lose its leaves in the fall, but keeps them throughout the year. If a tree is not evergreen it is called **deciduous**.

Extinction
The process of dying out. Animals that become extinct, such as dinosaurs, no longer exist. If an animal is **endangered**, often this means that it is threatened by extinction.

Global warming
An increase in temperature throughout the world. This is most likely due to the greenhouse effect, which is when heat becomes trapped in the Earth's atmosphere. Global warming leads to changes in weather conditions.

Habitat
The place where a particular animal or plant is usually found. Often an animal or plant will live in a certain habitat because several things about it suit them, such as the type of soil, temperature or amount of light.

Herd
A group of animals belonging to the same species that stick together in a large group.

Hibernation
A sleep-like state that some animals enter in order to survive cold winter months. When in hibernation, their body temperature, heart rate and breathing rate all drop. The animals are able to remain totally inactive for long periods of time, but stay alive.

Migration
The move that some animals make, usually in large groups, from one place to another. Animals often migrate in order to find food, warm weather, or to breed.

Nectar
The sweet juice of a plant, which often attracts insects or birds.

Pollen
Powdery substance made by plants that is carried by wind and insects to other plants to fertilize them.

Pollution
When harmful substances are released into the **environment**. Many different types of substances can cause environmental pollution.

Population
The total number of people or animals that live in a particular area or **habitat**.

Predator
An animal that captures, kills, and eats other animals. The animal that is caught by a predator is called the **prey**.

Prey
An animal hunted by another animal for food. The animal that hunts prey is called the **predator**.

Recycle
To treat materials in a certain way that makes them suitable to be used again. Many different materials can be recycled, such as glass, plastic, metal and paper.

Safari
A journey or adventure, often in Africa, and usually to find animals.

Species
A group of animals or plants that share the same characteristics. This means they may look similar, or behave in similar ways.

Venom
The poisonous fluid that some animals, such as snakes and spiders, release into their victims when they bite or sting. Venom is another word for poison.

Wingspan
The length of a bird's wings, from the tip of one wing to the tip of the other.

Web directory

If you want to discover more about the animals in this book and many more fascinating facts, then here is our pick of the best animal sites on the web.

www.nationalgeographic.com/kids
Discover fun facts, listen to animal sounds and download postcards and photographs of wild animals.

www.kidsgowild.com/kidsgowild/animalfacts
Wildlife news and conservation information on everything from aardvarks to zebras.

www.bbc.co.uk/nature/reallywild/amazing
Follow this A to Z guide to the world and meet some of the most amazing animals on each continent.

www.kidsplanet.org/factsheets/map.html
Factsheets with information on over 50 endangered animals from all over the world.

www.allaboutnature.com/biomes
Information about the animals that live in the Earth's many habitats, from deserts and grasslands to forests and ponds.

dsc.discovery.com/guides/animals/animals.html
Read the latest news about animals, explore the oceans and discover which animals would win an 'animal Olympics.'

www.wwf.org.uk/gowild
Includes sections on animals, habitats, games, cool stuff and how you can help to save the world's rare animals.

www.animalinfo.org
Information about endangered mammals and links to animal-related sites, organizations and publications.

www.seaworld.org/animal-info/animal-bytes
Factsheets with information about the conservation, ecology, classification and physical features of hundreds of animals.

Index

A
Acid rain 16
Albatross 43, 56
Alligator 13, 49
Ant
  army ant 21
  honeypot ant 32
  leafcutter ant 23
Anteater 56, 57
Antelope 31
Ass 31

B
Bat
  fruit bat 25
  long-eared bat 17, 55
  vampire bat 57
Bear
  American black bear 17
  Kodiak bear 54, 55
  polar bear 43
Beaver 13
Bee 28, 46
Beetle
  bombardier beetle 55
  dung beetle 29
  goliath beetle 54
  stag beetle 19
Blue jay 19
Bushbaby 20
Butterfly 55
  monarch butterfly 19
  morpho butterfly 22
  peacock butterfly 47
Butterfly fish 37

C
Cactus 31, 32
Cactus wren 32
Camel 30, 51, 55
Cat (domestic) 46
Centipede 55
Chamois 11
Cheetah 27
Chimpanzee 21
Chinchilla 11
Clam 37, 57
Clown fish 36
Condor 11
Cormorant 39
Cow 47
Crab 40
Crocodile 14, 56, 57
Crossbill 18
Cuckoo 19, 32

D
Deer
  elk 16
  fallow deer 17
  moose 16
  reindeer 45, 55
Dog 46
Dolphin 39, 52
Dormouse 17
Duck 14, 44

E
Eagle 11, 56
Eel 36
Elephant 27, 51, 56, 57

F
Falcon 54
Flamingo 15
Fly
  dragonfly 14, 54
  greenfly 47
  housefly 49, 57
  mayfly 57
Fox 57
  Arctic fox 45
  fennec fox 30
  red fox 49

G
Gibbon 21
Giraffe 27, 54
Global warming 42
Goat 11, 57
Golden lion tamarin 51
Goldfish 57
Gorilla 51
Grasshopper 28

H
Hamster 57
Hare 45
Hawfinch 56
Heron 14
Herring gull 39
Hippopotamus 13, 57
Horse 12, 47
Hummingbird 54, 56

I
Icefish 43

J
Jacana 56
Jackrabbit 31
Jaguar 20
Jellyfish 41

K
Kangaroo 25, 29, 56
Kestrel 49
Kingfisher 14
kookaburra 35
Kiwi 34
Koala 35

L
Ladybug 47
Lemur 35
Lion 27
Lionfish 37
Lizard
  chameleon 35, 57
  devil lizard 33
  gecko 47
  gila monster 31
  green iguana 22
  Komodo dragon 35
  marine iguana 35
Lobster 57

M
Manatee 13
Mandrill 25
Mallard 14
Manta ray 39
Marmot 55
Medicine 21, 52, 53
Mite 47
Monkey
  baboon 27
  Japanese macaque 10
  proboscis monkey 35
  spider monkey 21
  squirrel monkey 25
  tarsier monkey 21
Moth 55
Mouse 55
Mudskipper fish 15
Musk ox 45

N
Nutcracker 17

O
Octopus 37, 55
Orangutan 24
Ostrich 27, 28, 54, 55
Otter 13, 38
Owl
elf owl 33
snowy owl 45
tawny owl 18
Oystercatcher 39

P
Panda 11, 50
Pangolin 24
Parrot 57
hyacinth macaw 52
parakeet 32
scarlet macaw 22
Parrotfish 37
Partridge 56
Pelican 56
Penguin 42, 43
Pigeon 48
Pine tree 16
Platypus 13, 56, 57
Polyp 37
Porcupine 16
Porcupine fish 37
Possum 47
Puffin 39

Q
Quetzal 56

R
Rabbit 57
Raccoon 48
Rat 46, 31
Rhinoceros 27
black rhinoceros 53
white rhinoceros 55

S
Safari 27
Sailfish 54
Sand grouse 55
Sea anemone 36, 40
Sea dragon 37
Seahorse 40
Seal 38, 43
Sea lion 38
Shark 55
basking shark 54
great white shark 41
reef shark 37
whale shark 54, 57
Sheep 47
Shrew 57
Sloth 21, 54
Snake 57
anaconda 56
black-headed sea 55
emerald tree boa 23
gabon viper 56
rattlesnake 32
Snow goose 44
Snow leopard 10, 11, 51
Sparrow 48
Spider 55
Brazilian spider 55
goliath tarantula 21
Squirrel 17
Starfish 39, 40
Starling 46
Stork 46
Sugar glider 56

T
Tapir 25
Termite 21, 56
Tern 43
Tiger 24, 52, 57
Tortoise 34, 57
Toucan 22, 57
Tuatara 35
Turtle
green turtle 40
hawksbill turtle 39
leatherback turtle 53

V
Vulture 28

W
Walrus 43
Wasp 55
Weaverbird 28, 56
Whale 38
blue whale 53, 54, 56
humpback whale 39
killer whale 43, 57
sperm whale 39
Whip-poor-will 19
Wildebeest 26
Wolf 17
Wolverine 45
Woodpecker 18
Wrybill 56

Y
Yak 11, 55

Credits

Picture credits

A.N.T. Photo Library/NHPA: honeypot ant, page 32.

A.N.T. Photo Library/NHPA: sugar glider, page 56.

Arco Images/Alamy: spider monkey, page 21.

Arco Images/Alamy: crossbill, page 18.

Bob Elsdale/ The Image Bank/ Getty Images: dormouse, page 17.

David Fleetham/Alamy: blue whale, page 54.

Ellen McKnight/Alamy: leatherback turtle, page 53.

Fabrice Bettex/Alamy: great white shark, page 41.

Images and Stories/Alamy: proboscis monkey, page 35.

John Altringham: long-eared bat, page 17.

Jon Arnold Images/Alamy: kiwi, page 34.

Mark Carwardine/ NHPA: Yangtze River dolphin, page 52.

Mary McDonald/ Nature Picture Library: kangaroo rat, page 31.

Nicole Duplaix/National Geographic/ Getty Images: platypus, page 13.

Pete Oxford/ Robert Harding: pangolin, page 24.

Rick and Nora Bowers/Alamy: elf owl, page 33.